For Anna and Jeremy

My Thirty-Minute Bar Mitzvah

DENIS HIRSON has lived in France since 1975, yet has remained true to the title of one of his prose poems, 'The long distance South African'. Most of his books, both poetry and prose, are concerned with the memory of the apartheid years in South Africa. Two of his previous titles, *The House Next Door to Africa* and *I Remember King Kong (the Boxer)* were South African bestsellers.

DENIS HIRSON

My Thirty-Minute Minute Bar Mitzvah

A Memoir

PUSHKIN PRESS

Pushkin Press
Somerset House, Strand
London WC2R 1LA

The right of Denis Hirson to be identified as the author of this Work
has been asserted by him in accordance with the Copyright, Designs &
Patents Act 1988

My Thirty-Minute Bar Mitzvah was first published by Jacana Media
Pty in South Africa in 2022

First published by Pushkin Press in 2024

ISBN 13: 978-1-80533-753-9

Offset by Tetragon, London
Printed and bound in the United States of America

www.pushkinpress.com

9 8 7 6 5 4 3 2 1

Part One

The Lady with the Violet Hair

One

Of course I had a bar mitzvah.

It took place on a cool, crisp afternoon in Johannesburg on the day I turned thirteen, towards the end of August 1964.

There were three other people present, or five, depending on whom one chooses to include. Five, let's say, the men divided from the women according to the time-worn tradition.

There were no photographs, no gifts bought or made for the occasion; no singing or elevating sound, unless one counts the bellyfuls of steam rising up from the iron grid between the flagstones of the pavement across the road. But the steam hardly made a whisper and, anyway, I cannot be sure that I noticed it at all.

The ceremony lasted precisely thirty minutes, as had been agreed on well in advance, not a second longer. One of the people present announced the end in a voice as blunt as it was relieved.

Did I cross the threshold into manhood on that day, as one is, at least symbolically, supposed to do? I don't know. I doubt it. But I did at least in the wake of this event begin to understand a number of things I had not been confronted with before.

The person who might have been called my teacher would surely have wanted me to learn these lessons in an entirely different way, if I had to learn them at all, but there was no time beforehand, and not a moment left over at the end, to express any regret.

⁐

There was no Hebrew spoken during my bar mitzvah, nor did I read out aloud a portion of the consecrated biblical text. Everything happened in one language, or possibly two, but Hebrew was neither of them.

I already knew a number of Hebrew words, for example those that mean good morning and good night, peace, excuse me, please and thank you, boy and girl, water and prickly pear. I also knew that 'baruch' meant blessed, and that 'yael' meant ibex, which is a kind of goat. Those were the names of my parents, Baruch and Yael. I was the fruit of the union between a blessed one and a wild mountain goat, the first of their three children, the eldest by seven and a half years, and also the eldest grandchild on both sides.

As might be expected, 'baruch' is a holy word; it is also the beginning of many prayers. 'Baruch ata Adonai', Blessed art thou, Lord. I would have appreciated just a touch of holiness to add to proceedings during the thirty-minute ceremony, and why not even a prayer.

Someone might have raised a ladder of luminous words mounting rung by rung beyond the narrow, low-roofed confines where the occasion took place. This proved to be not only impossible but entirely unthinkable.

Several of my companions had already started learning Hebrew in preparation for their bar mitzvahs at the age of eleven or even earlier. On afternoons after school they disappeared behind the door of a room adjoining the newly built local orthodox shul, which stood like a sentinel among blocks of flats and scattered trees not three minutes from the school soccer field.

I watched them emerging an hour or so later as if they had been forcibly held under water, spluttering Hebrew syllables and exchanging jibes about their teacher, who was apparently no more than a doddering old clown.

Bevakakaka. Ani rotze, ani rotze, ani rotten tomatoes.

Bonded together in mockery they hopped around on the grass of the soccer field, the sound of their laughter rippling upwards like a single shared flag of belonging above their heads. Though they might have needed to exorcise from their bodies the boredom of their lessons, there was no question of their wanting to escape the ultimate goal: they would all end up having a bar mitzvah in shul one Saturday morning or another in the foreseeable future.

They would walk down the carpet with the eyes of the men and boys, as also the women and girls in the upper gallery, upon them. They would approach the raised lectern, passing row upon row of men wearing yarmulkes and draped in talliths, then stand at the sacred scroll and read from it to the congregation before being showered with gifts and adoration and going on to have a feast and make a speech in a marquee.

Such a procession of Jewishness they brought together before me, those boys: Stanley and JP, who was an orphan and once had ringworm; Colin who (accidentally, with a cricket ball) broke my front tooth; Jonny with the swimming pool at the bottom of his garden where Doris Day had dipped her shapely body one fabled afternoon.

There was Derek with his smooth raven-black hair and his violin; freckle-faced David; Peter of the hospitable mansion with a boxing bag swinging in the middle of the garden and a great cage of singing birds to one side; Boykie and his inexhaustible supply of jokes; Malcolm, Stephen, Ashley, Jacky whose house had recently been burgled; slothful, scheming Paul of the slack belly and bank-bags bloated with marbles.

Whatever has became of those boys, I wonder, every one of them from the plush and luxuriant, tree-lined northern suburbs of Johannesburg in the early 1960s?

Then again, was I not from the same suburbs, and Jewish too? What was so different about my family?

Well, we did live in the most ramshackle house on our block, with earthquake cracks across the inside walls, goose-pimpled plaster on the outside. And, unlike any of my friends' houses, ours was filled with almost nothing new.

As of the age of eight or nine I was out with my father, weekend after weekend, scouting for furniture in other people's homes: their inhabitants had fled the country in the wake of the Sharpeville massacre, the ensuing marches and violent repression of 1960. Added to this were the widely, luridly reported doings of the Mau Mau in Kenya. *The writing is on the wall for the whites*, went the rumour, and South Africa's airports and harbours were a hive of activity that year as, with anxious alacrity, white families packed up and left.

We, of course, were never going to leave. Not ever. My friends' parents might talk of buying a one-way ticket for London or Melbourne or New York, but not mine. And anyway we had just moved into our new antiquated house. So on a Saturday afternoon my father and I would add ourselves to a little crowd following a well-fed auctioneer about from room to stripped room of what had once been an absent stranger's stately abode. After a few hours we drove back home to proudly lay our loot before my mother: Kilim carpets, a pinewood Swedish desk, lamps, vases, kitchenware, imbuia armchairs, a Morris settee dotted with little maroon roses.

At first the effect of all these things, once installed, was somewhat theatrical, like a stage set for what really stole the limelight in our house: books. I knew no one else whose house was filled with as many books, pushing their way up from the pinewood floors to the moulded ceilings; books with my parents' first names inscribed inside them, looped together and underlined in my father's meticulous script, Baruch & Yael, as if this were both their joint fortune and the contract of their togetherness.

Our garden, too, was different. The grass was as worn as a moth-eaten cloth, the flowerbeds lacking in that lush, perky look that comes with constant care. We had a gardener, but he was absent for weeks on end, a withdrawn, soft-spoken man who may well have been involved in some kind of political activity. On several occasions I saw my father speaking to him quietly around the back of the house; perhaps he was eventually arrested. Whatever the case, he finally disappeared, after which the grass was gradually worn even thinner than before.

But never mind the state of the grass, or the surfeit of books, or our adopted furniture. We were from the same suburbs as all my friends even if it felt as if we weren't.

And what about the fact of being Jewish?

That was a secret which I myself could not crack.

From an early age I was somehow made aware that sharing this secret with strangers might possibly be dangerous. But it was also not to be spoken of within the walls of our own house, despite the fugitive signs that Jewishness was very much a part of our lives.

Take my father's whistling, for example. In the late afternoon or evening he would come home from the university where he was a physics lecturer, walk through the front door and whistle, the same six brief, sharp notes ending with a seventh long one every time. In answer to this call my mother, if she was already back from medical school, would emerge from wherever she had been to greet him.

They had told me where this whistling tune came from: Hashomer Hatzair, the youth movement better known to them as 'HH'. As a boy I learned, without really understanding, that 'HH' was Zionist and therefore Jewish, as well as socialist, and was one strand of the bond between them since they had both been members.

But when they mentioned this, which was not often, the Zionist part was passed over in silence and the Jewish part went mysteriously missing, like a piece of an almost completed jigsaw puzzle that is found to be lost, whose shape can clearly be guessed at but unfortunately not filled.

I knew it was there, hidden somewhere out of sight, but the words for it were not available to me.

Why was this so?

I did not know, nor did I try and find out.

Perhaps that was simply the way things were.

Perhaps I had, or made sure I had, other things on my mind, such as catching a new kind of beetle for my beetle collection, or boiling another golf-ball. The people next door sometimes chipped a golf-ball into our back garden, and I boiled it, slicing off the dimpled outer resin skin and cutting through the densely meshed rubber thread below to get to the bag of yellowish gel hidden in the middle.

That tiny bag was a sort of secret, and I liked secrets. I was a solitary child, and secrets were part of the way I kept to myself. There were lots of them in the stories I read, they were what made me turn to the next page. They had power, but only as long as they were not yet revealed. In other words, you had to know about their existence, though their inner meaning might remain elusive for a considerable amount of time.

Like Jewishness.

If I was the least bit curious about it then I buried

my curiosity. I did not want any angry answers entering the quietness of my world. And vaguely, distantly, I sensed that if I asked the wrong question then anger would come rumbling forth from my father, though I hardly knew why.

There were also other secrets in our house, and I definitely knew I should not ask about them. I don't know whether I needed any proof that these particular secrets had power. But, as if I did, there came a day when one of them exploded, and then nothing was ever the same again.

For all my solitariness, or more likely because of it, I badly wanted to play sport at school, especially in a team: sport was something that could easily be shared with my classmates in the long blue hours after school. The only problem being that I was a lousy sportsman.

But I was lucky. One fateful afternoon out on our school soccer field when our coach, Mr Spoor, was choosing boys for the under-ten team, he told me to go and stand between the goalposts. *Jump*, said Mr Spoor, kicking the ball to one side.

I jumped.

This is one of two very different moments that come immediately to mind when I think of sport at primary school: the big moment of inner brightness when I flexed my knees, pushed myself upwards, and in the resulting airborne state was so amazed to find the ball securely in my outstretched hands that I did not even feel the bump when I landed.

A few more kicks, a few more saves and I received the coveted pale blue jersey that meant I was the goalie in the school team. This was all the more remarkable since the other positions on the field were definitely beyond my reach. I could run all right, but when it came to dribbling, passing and shooting, either my boots did not find the ball or, when they did, the ball clearly had intentions of its own.

Goalkeeping was different. Most of the time you just had to stop the ball, not get involved in the business of furthering its intricate, obstacle-filled journey to the far side of the field. And if ever your body left the ground in order to intercept the ball's trajectory, the ground was sure to be there when you came back down.

This explains why I preferred soccer to swimming. The problem with swimming was all the water. It was fine to float on a lilo in the sun, but what was the point of putting your face into the water so that it masked your face and rushed through your mouth and nostrils as urgently as if they were plugholes? Wouldn't it just have been easier to breathe in the fresh air while walking *around* the pool if you had to get to the other side?

I was never going to be selected to represent our school at swimming, but, like all the others who were not in the team, I had to go along when there was an inter-school gala. This unfortunately brings me to the second moment I think of when it comes to sport at primary school, because there was just such a gala in progress one late morning in northern Johannesburg, at the Zoo Lake Municipal Swimming Bath.

Doing breaststroke down their lanes in the rippling silver-blue jelly of the pool were seven or eight girls in shiny skins and costumes and plastic swimming caps, water parting neatly before their dipping, rising faces. All around them, various school war cries erupted from among the children packing the stands.

And at the top of one of those stands a group of us, deciding that it must be time to eat, took out our lunch boxes and opened our home-made, wax-paper-wrapped contents; all, that is, except for one boy who had forgotten to bring his sandwiches with him. *Ops us a sarmie*, he requested of no one in particular, and, from the place immediately in front of him where I happened to be sitting, I handed back one of my mother's offerings.

There was a pause, and then the sandwich was returned to me with a single fatal bite missing. *It isn't kosher*, the boy announced so that everyone could hear each syllable that came shooting with burning intensity in my direction. I was filled with sudden inner darkness, though my face must have been flaming red.

That boy, inside-left in our soccer team, third or fourth in our class after Leonie Hofmeyr who always came first and was right then busy winning the race down in the shaken-up waters of the pool; that boy, soon to be one of the bar mitzvah boys at the local shul, had, at least in my eyes, instantaneously turned into the representative of an entire group, a tightly bonded community several generations deep now massed against me with a flock of furrowed brows angled in my direction.

Who did I imagine all those people to be? Prominent among them were not only the Jewish children at our school but also members of their families. I had seen them often enough at the side of the soccer field supporting their sons, later driving away in spacious, gleaming cars. I had myself been ferried to and from matches in those same cars, by mothers who had slow voices and tea parties and all the time in the world. I had exchanged occasional distant glances with the fathers who also pitched up at matches once in a while, wearing rings and glittery ties with tie-pins, stretching their smiles between plump, immobile cheeks.

I had even been welcomed into some of their big, spotless homes; out on their verandas I had been waited upon by servants wearing starched white livery. But now because of my unkosher sandwich I felt their indignant collective presence come pressing in on all sides until I became the accused in a court case, certain that the Jewish boys up there in the stands were busy passing judgment on me.

How could it be otherwise, since even inside me there were elusive, latent forces of ancestry at work, pressures for which I could barely find a name? My mind went numb and my tongue stalled as, with no alibi to call on, I faced the irrefutable charge of transgression.

There, right under my nose, was the unJewish evidence against me: my unsuspecting mother's sandwich. It consisted of two fresh slices of brown Atlas bread filled with succulent roast veal and rosemary and fine slices of cucumber. It was also unmistakably and irreparably lined with butter.

☞

My classmates and I were ten or eleven years old and it was 1961, the year after the Sharpeville massacre.

Dr Verwoerd, the prime minister, had declared a republic, which meant that we had to go to the school hall and learn to sing the national anthem, in English as well as Afrikaans, with our teacher, Mrs Miles, sitting at the piano. She had straight hair dyed henna-red and arranged as neatly as a wig over her head with a fringe in front; sometimes in class she asked her pet pupil to comb it. She also had dyed eyebrows and big cheeks and the tops of her arms wobbled when she played.

A new young teacher called Mr Reineke, who dressed very smartly and kept flicking his glossy quiff out of his eyes, stood on the stage using both hands to conduct our singing as if he were directing the traffic. Earlier in the year he had tried to teach us to sing the Lord's Prayer in the same way, but once again our efforts did not please him in the least, so we had to start several times over. *Ringing out from our blue heavens, Uit die blou van onse hemel.*

Blou, insisted Mr Reineke, opening his mouth wide and describing an O as wide as a hula-hoop with his arms while Mrs Miles asked a boy in the front row to go and fetch her another glass of water.

My father definitely disliked Dr Verwoerd and told me not to go to school on Republic Day when we were all supposed to receive a little national flag and a medal, but Mrs Miles kept them for me anyway.

Soon, because of the republic, we had freshly minted money in our pockets when standing in line at the school tuck-shop at break. Gone was the brown one-penny coin showing on one side the demure British queen, Elizabeth II Regina. She had recently also been our queen, or almost our queen, but now she definitely wasn't.

On the other side used to be an old sailing ship that

might have brought her ancestors across the ocean to our shores. But on the new one-cent coin, which was yellowish and sat so lightly in the palm of the hand that it felt like play money, the ship had been replaced by an ox-wagon, one belonging to the Voortrekkers whom, we learned, had once upon a time come trekking northwards from the Cape, singing songs and shooting at lions and tribes.

As for the Queen, she had been replaced by Jan van Riebeeck from Holland. There he was in his lace collar and moustache and wavy waterfall of hair, just as he had been on landing in his ship in 1652, the first man ever to set foot on the shores of the Cape, we were told, only to be met by a straggly little crowd of Bushmen.

UNITY IS STRENGTH, EENDRAG MAAK MAG was written in capital letters on the coin all the way around Van Riebeeck's dapper bust. This meant that he and I had something in common: if unity was important to him then it was to me, too, at least to a certain degree.

Whatever the content of my sandwiches, I wasn't British, nor was I an Afrikaner. I *was* in fact one of the Jewish boys in the class, wasn't I, even if only because I wasn't anything else. And though I might not know what exactly this meant to me, I hardly wanted to stick out among the others like an unkosher thumb.

I had shared one of my mother's scrumptious sandwiches with a boy I had thought of as a sort of friend. As a result that boy now had a problem because, sitting all the way at the top of the packed stands in the middle of a swimming gala, he had to find somewhere to spit out his polluted mouthful.

I spoke to no one about this incident, but it stuck inside me like a splinter and would not go away. How could I invite a Jewish boy over to our house if there was going to be problems about the food served at mealtimes?

So I turned to Barry.

Barry played centre-half in our school soccer team, a pivotal position for a skilful player. Everyone liked him. He was crack at marbles, too. He had a finely drawn face, a soft voice, and he was not Jewish. I asked him over, and was in turn invited to his place. We played soccer with Barry's brother out in the garden, as well as our version of French cricket, with an upturned tomato crate for a wicket. We sat at the kitchen table and did our homework together.

One summer Barry's family invited me to their farm. For the first time I saw a sheep with its belly cut open and gut spilling out khaki-green into the dust of the yard. I was taught to use a pellet-gun, then shot at a bird to prove I could do it. And at some point I said something against another boy in our class, remarking that it would be difficult to invite *him* to the farm: *he*, after all, would only eat kosher food.

Years later, that same boy, a young man by then, paid me a visit and reminded me sharply of what I had said. All three of us had been friends, hadn't we? Good friends. And with the shield of my need and the knife of my uncertainty I had betrayed one of us, wanting the other to myself, seeking out a territory where I could draw closer to someone my age despite the unspoken, bristling contradictions that surrounded me.

Badly needing the company of one boy, I had stood on a second one to reach him, denying the fact that he, too, was a friend, and also that we were both of the same lineage.

Two

Being Jewish was one thing. Having something to do with Israel was quite another: Israel was always in my vicinity, or not altogether, like a person who hadn't yet rung the doorbell, or had rung it but was somewhere else when you opened the door. Israel was a country unlike any of the others because it wasn't only on the map, nor in the end was it just outside the house. It had mysteriously already come in and was right in the middle of people's lives.

For a start, there were the Keren Kayemet boxes, especially in the neighbourhood, some distance from our own, where my father's parents, Granny Lily and Grandpa Joe, lived.

The boxes were blue and white, made of tin, about the size of a fat book, with a sort of spring (I thought) around the inside of the slot at the top so as (I supposed) to prevent anyone from trying to get the money out (I never tried). They were often placed at the entrance to houses, next to the black Bakelite telephone, or propping up a set of dog-eared thrillers on a shelf. If you put some money into the slot then it would go to Israel and trees would be able to grow there.

How exactly this happened I could not work out. In the first place I had never seen anyone actually come to take the boxes away, or, for that matter, bring them back again. Nonetheless, I checked that they were sometimes filled and sometimes empty, which meant that there were mysterious hands reaching into people's houses to get them because of the trees.

Why trees, I wondered? Why not spend at least some of the money on a cake mixer for Granny Lily, for example, since she could really do with a new one?

I supposed that there weren't any trees in Israel, or hardly any. Maybe the whole country was bald, and people had to stand at the side of the sea waiting for ships to bring in the trees they so badly needed.

Could a shilling or even half a crown really help to buy one?

Granny Lily's Keren Kayemet box was on a low, almost marble, veined beige mantelpiece above the electric heater in the living room; a troop of ebony elephants with ivory tusks went marching all the way up to it, the biggest elephant in front and a baby one with tiny tusks bringing up the rear. Mr and Mrs Goodman next door also had a box and so did Mr Harrison a few gates down, but that was before his wife died and he left and his house had to be fumigated.

Mr Goodman was a bar mitzvah teacher and he had a piano that occupied a whole room. A few of the keys were a bit brown at the edges like smokers' fingers.

Sometimes, I would be near the tall brick wall that separated my grandmother's yard from the Goodmans' house, spending a long time listening to what was going on in there. Sunlight sharpened the bits of broken bottle stuck in the cement at the top of the wall, while from the other side came the sound of a boy's voice diligently following Mr Goodman's instructions, up and down the piano notes on the way to his bar mitzvah.

Mr Goodman's son Hershey had already had one. Afterwards, he started wearing a leather jacket to go with his ducktail hairstyle, but now everything was all right because he was in Israel, which was where you went.

Granny Lily and I walked across to Mr and Mrs Goodman's at tea-time and were invited into the kitchen to see the wonder of neon tubes against the ceiling: they went plink, plink, plink while they were switching on, letting out a pale, pinkish-orange mist of light. Over tea, Mr Goodman asked me if I was going to have a bar mitzvah and when I said nothing because I didn't know what to say, Mr Goodman glanced at Granny Lily. She glanced back at him sharply from under her perm and changed the subject.

But the question hovered over me, just out of reach. Nor did Granny Lily bring it any closer by talking about it when we were alone. She surely had other things on her mind, such as what to make her husband for supper, or when she could take the tram into town and buy a pattern with which to sew a new dress for herself. And anyway, the bar mitzvah question was linked not only to me but to my parents, and she studiously avoided talking about them except once, when we were walking alongside the park on the way back to her place from the shops.

I don't remember how the conversation began, but I do remember that just for once Granny Lily became extremely angry. I also remember how it ended, because she said they were a pair of well-educated donkeys. Then she changed the subject.

When both my parents were busy, which was often enough, I spent days and nights staying over at Granny Lily's home, having meals with her and Grandpa Joe, wandering across to the park to play soccer or fly a kite.

Sometimes people came over to visit Granny Lily, or she occasionally visited them and took me with her. They were mainly family members and a few neighbours, with blue-rinsed perms and dress patterns in special packets, cigarette holders, talcum-powdered cheeks and bones that shrank, which was what Granny Lily said happened when you grew old.

They had a great many things to speak about in English and also in Yiddish, especially when I came too close, and they drank their tea black with grape jam swirling in it. *Purl one slip one*, they repeated like a private prayer, knitting and crocheting and talking away.

I hung around for a while, but soon went off to start reading through the comics I had brought with me, following the adventures of Archie and Veronica and Jughead, Richie Rich the Poor Little Rich Boy, Bugs Bunny, Beetle Bailey, Popeye and Olive, Casper the Friendly Ghost, Little Lotta and Felix the Cat.

I read till my mind was thin as a page and all the quirky doings blurred into each other; I read till the words were pressed out of their bubbles and went on speaking in my mind. I closed the last comic and still Elmer Fudd would be tiptoeing around muttering *Be vewy, vewy quiet, I'm hunting wabbits*, while Tweety Bird repeated *I tawt I taw a puddy tat*.

So I went to revive myself with a cold strawberry milkshake and a plateful of pastries: crisp, airy waves of sweetness, balls sticky with black molasses, tender diamonds of carrot and ginger, soft, rolled mouthfuls of cinnamon, even their names were waiting to be eaten: kichel, teiglach, imberlach, rugelach.

Granny Lily spoke Yiddish and her pastries had tasty names, that was how things were. Comic books were where you went when there was nowhere else to go. And trees didn't have to stay in one place. They would be planted thanks to all the coins in those blue and white boxes in Johannesburg, miles and miles of trees floating for a great distance till they could take root in the land of Israel, which was out of sight yet so close you could almost see it.

I don't remember seeing any Keren Kayemet boxes in our part of Johannesburg, though there must have been some. Nor did I notice many women with perms, though there must have been more. The people who lived in our neighbourhood were generally much younger, they swam in pools before sipping sundowners and held tennis parties on Sundays.

As for our family, I remember my pale-skinned mother doggy-paddling with some effort across the width of someone else's pool (my swimming skills no doubt come from her). My father had severe gout and his form of exercise was walking, usually in deep discussion with another man.

There were also meetings at our house, behind closed doors because of the bug in the Bakelite telephone at the far end of the passage. Everyone smoked till the windows clouded over, but they did not drink. All we had in the way of alcohol was half a cheap bottle of cooking wine in the kitchen.

Nonetheless, there we were, perched on a corner of a block on the smart side of the city, in a house different from my friends' houses. In a suburb unlike the one where my grandparents lived.

In fact, for me the whole of Johannesburg was split in two.

There were no jaded blocks of flats very near us as there were across the road from Granny Lily and Grandpa Joe's. The houses were bigger and did not look like each other. None that I knew of had meagre lines of daisies and foxgloves standing in a little strip of garden out in front.

There weren't mezuzahs on all the doorposts in our part of Johannesburg.

There wasn't an ordinary house that had been turned into a shul.

Shops didn't display rows of tongue that was grey and almost blue; pimply, juicy pickled cucumbers and gefilte fish and kneaded, honey-coloured kitke and hamantaschen with their hidden, tender nests of poppy seeds.

There was no Mr Squire standing at the doorway of Squire's Outfitters with a smile under his luxuriant moustache and row upon row of suits hanging flat as shadows behind him, waiting for men to come in with their wives and fill them out. They would remove their hats, lift their jackets like sea-birds about to take off and have their waists tape-measured by the ever-ready

Mr Squire. If there was someone like him on our side of the city, I never had the opportunity to find out.

Mr Squire would have been one of the people in favour of my having a bar mitzvah, especially when Granny Lily went to his shop and was considering buying me my first and only suit, one with a chocolate and black hound's tooth pattern. Finally she did buy it, which was fortunate because I had started going to parties with girls in them and suits were what you had to put on.

I wish you well to wear it, said Granny Lily, all the weight of worry in her face lifting for just a moment with the pleasure of giving me something I had been wanting for ages.

I went to a few parties wearing the suit, wondering how to avoid the shoes of the girl whom I had somehow managed to get to dance with me, and what to do with her once the music slowed down. But at least I had a suit, and vaguely supposed I would be able to wear it later for my bar mitzvah because Mr Squire had already shown Granny Lily how she could let out the waist and lengthen the legs in case I grew.

As things turned out, I did not wear the suit on that occasion. Its existence did not even enter my mind, I had a number of other things to think about. And anyway, there would not have been the time or place to change into it on the day in question.

It is worth mentioning here some of the guests who

might have come to my bar mitzvah, all of them living more or less on Granny Lily's side of the city: Granny Lily's sisters Essie and Eva; her sister-in-law Bessie and a few people on that side of the family; Granny Lily's sons Norman, Innes and Eric, who were, after all, my father's brothers despite the bad blood (never spoken of and never explained) between them. However unlikely their presence would have been, I had already spent quite a lot of time with them, so they might have considered coming, especially Norman and Eric whom I knew better.

I had watched them getting taller, plump and then plumper, smashing at Jokari balls and squash balls; whooshing around a municipal swimming pool under the floodlights at night like great pink, hairy seals during games of water polo; rolling around on beds in Lily's house behind almost closed doors over the weekend, this way and that, with girlfriends who eventually turned into wives.

If my uncles had come, their wives would have accompanied them, along with a few new gurgling offspring.

Granny Lily's maid Martha would have come. She was always there, feudally faithful, plucking and singeing chickens, polishing furniture, at the edge of the frozen sea of emotion that stretched between Granny Lily and Grandpa Joe.

And of course Granny Lily herself.

But neither Granny Lily, nor any of the other people mentioned above, came to my bar mitzvah.

They couldn't, because they were not invited.

No one put them on the guest list.

There was no guest list in the first place.

There were no guests.

⁓

Surely Grandpa Joe would not have come to my bar mitzvah, even had he been invited. No amount of cajoling from Granny Lily could have brought him there.

Grandpa Joe lies somewhere at the bottom of this story like an ancient fish in the darkness of deep waters, occupying far more space than anyone would have credited him with, since he spent his days perfecting the sorry art of not being there.

By day he was washed up in a seaweed-coloured armchair in a corner of Granny Lily's living room, behind stacked issues of *Popular Science* and the *Reader's Digest*. Wind might blow the chiffon curtain across his bald head while the giant fern above him delicately shivered all the way to the tips of its dimpled leaves; he just sat there and none of my antics would distract him.

Once in a while he went over to his workshop on the other side of the dank yard with a toaster or a wireless that had been broken and brought over for repairs. I followed him in, watching from a discreet distance as he went to his worktable.

There were giant coils of metal and wire strung from the ceiling, sunrays glittering with dust high above his squat, bent form, his soldering iron making a small circle of molten light in the low layers of gloom. But however close I came he did not turn towards me, hardly glancing in my direction when Granny Lily called out and it was time for him to troop back in his one-man army across the yard for brisket and fruit salad.

Grandpa Joe's silence filled the whole house. The voices from Springbok Radio went through it like a spoon dipping into a dish full of jelly that smoothed over straight afterwards. If the doorbell or telephone rang he wouldn't budge. All Granny Lily got in answer to a question was a grunt, which is what I got when I wanted him to give me the stamps on old envelopes while he was looking through his accounts at the passage cupboard.

A begrudging noise came out of him, almost a cough, and a couple of those stamps were reluctantly passed over to me, for example the sixpenny ones with their image of oranges like light bulbs on a triangular tree, and that was that. Soon Grandpa Joe was back, one grumpy step after the next, taking position behind his trench of magazines, or before the cards with which he played patience on the glass cover of the pitch-brown weighty table that took up much of the living room.

Behind his trench and almost ready to explode.

But at Pesach, when his sons came over with their wives and young children, he was a very different man. Just for that evening he stepped out of the valley of the shadow of depression in a clean white shirt.

How unusually relaxed Grandpa Joe was, sitting in his short body at the far end of the table, while Granny Lily and Martha entered bearing a steaming tureen of shiny chicken soup and a bowl of the most succulent kneidelach. And where had he discovered that smile all of a sudden, as he lifted off the plate of matzah the white tasselled cloth from Jerusalem with the Tower of David printed on it, and muttered a prayer? How could he possibly be speaking serenely like that to all my uncles, with the sun lighting up his face though it was well past nightfall?

I would be sitting at the far end of the table, without my mother or younger brother (my sister had not yet been born). My father was not there either. Never once had I seen him enter that house.

But why?

It was impossible for me to even consider that my father might have done anything wrong. So could Grandpa Joe have been at fault? I did not know. But between the two of them the city was divided, and this was the real reason why for me it was split in two. An invisible, jagged crack ran down the middle of it and went right through me, too.

But why?

No one spoke about all this.

It was another secret.

I sat there quietly, Granny Lily bending specially towards me as she dished out the gefilte fish.

Was I not the eldest son of her favourite son who no longer passed through her door, and was I not also the message of conciliation he sent her? I sat there in the house from which he had been exiled, listening once again to the Passover story.

Moses wanted Pharaoh to let his people go because they had to sweat all day building pyramids and sphinxes. But Pharaoh wouldn't. Even when the rivers turned to blood and all the fish died and the rivers stank and there was no water to drink. Frogs came hopping into the houses and bedchambers, and the dust of the earth turned into lice; there was a great black cloud of flies; all the cattle of Egypt died and the skin of the Egyptians broke out in boils.

But each time the Lord hardened Pharaoh's heart and he said no, even when hail struck man and beast and every herb of the field and locusts came with the east wind and chewed through everything that remained and the world was covered in darkness.

Then the people of Israel sacrificed a lamb and

painted their doorposts with its blood. And seeing this, the angel of death arched up its shadowy wings and passed over their homes and instead visited the Egyptians, and killed each firstborn son.

By the time Moses and his people had crossed the Red Sea with some matzah in their pockets and were on their way to the Promised Land, most of my very young cousins had already fallen asleep. Soon afterwards, my uncles were once again happily chatting to Grandpa Joe while my aunts helped Granny Lily and Martha clear up the dishes and I waited to be driven home by my Great-Aunt Essie.

There, finally, was her motorcar, parked out under the plane trees in the night, with its rubber running boards and headlamps like praying mantis eyes, and the comfortable smell of leather and Rothmans filter-tipped cigarettes inside.

I leaned back in my seat with the street lamps streaming past overhead, and started distractedly singing a tune I had heard on the wireless. I stretched and kneaded it together with bits of the music my father listened to on the gramophone, then changed it again until I had a long solo song of my own.

That was by Johann Sebastian Bach, I announced to my great-aunt when it was over.

Mhmmm, she responded after a very pensive moment as we went steering through the night.

And like the burned but still glowing end of a

matchstick my grandfather's smile followed me from across the Pesach table, but it flickered and bent and turned black before I managed to get to sleep.

⁓

Something had once happened to Grandpa Joe, I found out years later, something which in turn entered my father's bloodstream in an invisible burning vessel and came down to me, even as far as the circumstances of my bar mitzvah. But what exactly was it that he went through in the month of October 1922, not much more than a year after his marriage to Granny Lily?

There, you can see them together in a photograph on Muizenberg beach: they are on their honeymoon, staying in one of the cheaper hotels not too far from the sea.

She could be slightly distressed, but perhaps that is just a strong breeze against her face as she holds down her dark hair and frowns, her other hand bearing a straw hat crowned with flowers before her like a shield. Joe stands close by, dapper and suave, with what might be a victorious smile and one white shoe in the ambit of her flounced dress.

I doubt they'll be going out for lunch, there is not much money, and a wicker picnic basket sits to one side on the sand. Money may have been part of the problem, because certain members of Lily's family thought a lowly electrician was not good enough for her. But was that the full story?

Here they are again in Johannesburg with my nine-month-old father. In one photograph Lily glows, buxom and easy with little Baruch perched next to her on a chair; in another, Joe cups his son's chubby thigh, holding him up wet-cheeked and restless before the camera.

Pride is what Joe's face shows, the flushed look of a young man who has married an attractive woman from a Latvian shtetl nearby his own and founded a family with her; a soft if ill-secured nest in a country of refuge that neither of them knows very well, but at least they are alive and well in the sunshine.

Not the least sign, as Joe raises his son aloft for posterity, that in a matter of weeks he would be gone.

But he was.

Out the door, to my knowledge no one to this day has revealed where he went, nor was he back for a very long time.

⁀

It has been impossible for me to discover the why and wherefore of Grandpa Joe's story.

Perhaps it all began with pure domestic frustration: chicken soup on the dinner table that had gone greasy cold while Lily sat in the bedroom with baby Baruch at her breast; there she was, lovingly cradling him, while she had barely responded to Joe's advances since Baruch's birth.

Dvorah, Joe's battle-axe of a mother-in-law, staying over at the time, may have made it clear all over again that she wanted a finer match for her pretty youngest daughter.

There could have been some remark so small that Joe hardly saw it slipping its way under his skin: perhaps a broken toaster at breakfast time and Dvorah commenting that he was not even capable of fixing the appliances in his own home.

Perhaps there was more. Dizzying debt after Joe had been tricked into helping to fund some conman's get-rich-quick moneymaking scheme. Or trouble at work, Joe choking on his words and shaking his fist when a dissatisfied client threatened to take him to court.

The atmosphere in Johannesburg was still taut and edgy in the aftermath of the miners' strike earlier that year. Joe and Lily, living in Jeppe, south-west of the middle of town, had most probably heard the police rattling past on horseback and bombs dropping from low-flying planes; a commando of strikers could have stopped Joe from going out to work.

No meat, no newspapers for weeks. WORKERS OF THE WORLD, UNITE AND FIGHT FOR A WHITE SOUTH AFRICA read the banner of those marching down the street. Joe no doubt knew the white miners did not want to lose their jobs to cheap black labour, and he, too, was a worker. But was he really one of them? He may have been a worker of the world, but was he of *their* world, and could he take sides in such a dispute?

Had he not fled Latvia to get away from the guns and blood in the streets? During the events of 1922, right there in Johannesburg and the nearby mining towns at least 200 strikers were killed and one thousand injured. In October, three strike leaders were sent to the gallows.

That month, after Joe had slammed the door of his home behind him, he could have heard men discussing such things loudly in one of those rowdy, smoky honky-tonk bars he walked past, the whole place packed solid and steaming with soldiers and pimps, tradesmen, merchants and layabouts. But he would not even have considered pushing open the swing-doors, stranger that he was to every one of them in the strangeness of this land.

So where did he go?

Wherever it was, when he returned home Lily had left, taking Baruch with her to stay with relatives, and would have nothing to do with him.

Then what?

So much could have happened to a young despairing immigrant in the scarred city, trenches not yet filled in after the strike, electrical wires sliced open like the veins of a suicide case wherever he might have gone, Jeppe or Fordsburg, Boksburg, Benoni, Brakpan. There was enough work for him to last a lifetime.

People had come flooding into town from the drought-ridden interior of the country, poor whites and poorer blacks, men still hobbling around on wartime crutches, widow after young widow dressed in mourning.

Could one of them have tempted him?

After a month or two in a rooming house, life at home alone being unbearable to him.

Did he finally soften under that surly carapace of his, or was it only later that he turned so crusty and mute?

No one knows what really happened to him, but he was reunited with his wife and child all right.

Four years later.

Brought himself to Baruch's school, all spruced up in a suit together with pince-nez, collar and tie, and took his son in his arms at the railing of the fence.

It was 1925 or '26.

He had three more sons with Lily, but the rift between them never healed. Divorce was not a ready option. So instead they settled for cold tolerance; moved together into a house where the rooms were bigger, and still there was not enough air for either of them. Lily ran the household, with Baruch stoutly on her side against Joe.

Once, in the early 1980s, entirely out of the blue, my father confided in me, a baffled expression on his face: *I am sixty years old now. Will I ever stop hating my father?*

If only I had been able to ask him then what had weighed so oppressively between them.

If only I had been able to think, then, of their relationship, and also of what it might mean to our family.

Plague in the sap of the tree of ancestry.

Joe, it seems, was rarely able to shake himself out of the captivity he had devised for himself, at least not in my presence. He would return home from work day after day in silence, fitting his sullen face to an open, well-thumbed back copy of *Popular Science* or *Reader's Digest.*

He surely never heard what my mother's family had to say about him when he visited them in Israel in the 1950s.

Such a sweet man, they said. Always smiling as he sat out in the sunlight.

Like a bird let out of a cage.

Israel never entered our house in a Keren Kayemet

box. But it came all the same, mostly in aerogrammes, which I at the age of eight or nine thought were a very bad idea: instead of a stamp on an envelope, aerogrammes only had a drawing of an aeroplane in a corner of the rectangular fold of blue paper, nothing at all that could be floated off the surface and added to my stamp collection or used for swaps.

The aerogrammes usually came from England, to which friends of my parents had disappeared, leaving a gap in our lives. But once every few weeks my mother's mother, who lived in Israel, used to send one to her, with a few words added in at the end from her father.

I had never met these grandparents, which was one less reason for me to feel any enthusiasm about the arrival of their letters, but my mother was overjoyed.

Here she came now, not exactly walking, she never had two feet firmly on the ground – but streaking headlong through the front door – starched white coat from medical school lifted in flight, lipstick shining, stockings showing black seams down the back of her legs; briefcase meeting the floorboards, face lighting up as she discovered the aerogramme.

Soon she was sitting at the kitchen table reading it to my father and me, speaking words full of squelchy music, since they were in Yiddish, so I had to wait for my mother's translation, and even then most of it was beyond me.

My mother's voice rose and broke into giggles as if she were going down the high slide in the park, getting younger with every word, half in the kitchen and half off to the land of Israel.

That was surely where my mother's parents wanted her to be. Why else would they go on sending us not only aerogrammes but also the array of gifts the postman delivered on other occasions? These gifts, however, produced exactly the opposite effect to the aerogrammes, because neither of my parents seemed to want to have anything to do with them.

There was a paper-napkin rack, an ornamental cover for a matchbox, a little candlestick holder, all of them made of beaten brass; a tooled leather book-cover, a tasselled cloth just like the one that covered Grandpa Joe's matzah at the Pesach table. They were all mementoes from the land of Israel, and they bore Hebrew letters as well as English words naming the places portrayed on them: The Old City, The Tower of David, The Wailing Wall, The Lion's Gate.

In our house there was a room between rooms, you went down the passage to the kitchen through its dimly lit width but nothing actually happened there. So it turned into a sort of attic since we didn't have one, and there my grandparents' gifts gathered dust, till I did with them what I knew full well I should not do.

Diagonally opposite our house, just up the road,

there lived a woman named Mrs McDonald.

I had met her one afternoon when I came knocking at her door, wanting to sell her a raffle ticket from my school. She invited me in to have a glass of cold Nesquik, something I had never tasted before except in the Greek grocery store where, laid out on a table at the door, there were tiny sample cups of this miraculous, sweet powder that dissolved instantly in milk after being stirred, all brand new and sparkly with chocolate-coated bubbles.

After that, I visited Mrs McDonald quite a few times in the afternoon when school was over. She was broad and matronly and mild, with a round, soft face. Her kitchen always smelled of baking. Sometimes, when she sat me down at the Formica table in there, she gave me some of her flapjacks, or a slice of sponge cake with crisp, acidulous lemon icing.

She was a kind of temporary Granny Lily on our side of the city.

I wanted to give her something in return. So, one by one, I took away the gifts that had been sent to us from Israel, and presented them to her.

Here you are, Mrs McDonald, I might have said.
This was from my mother's parents to my mother.
They love her.
She loves them, too.
But she doesn't know what to do about them being in the land of Israel. Do you?

I like being in your long, cosy kitchen, Mrs McDonald. It feels a bit like a boat.

My mother's not around much. She's a medical student. Have you seen her whizzing past in her white coat on the way to the bus stop?

Anyway, here is a present.

Can I come back?

That's what my grandparents sent these presents for in the first place, so my mother would come back.

This is one of them.

Now it's for you.

I don't think you should tell her.

Thanks again for the flapjacks.

And for sitting with me for so long without finding something else to do.

Thanks for just sitting there and listening to me for a while, Mrs McDonald.

There were no candles for my thirteenth birthday, and no cake to stick them into.

No one sang 'Happy Birthday' with my name as part of the song. Nor was this a problem, since the occasion was hardly about me.

There was, however, some hot tea, which I badly needed, and a few plates of sandwiches and sweetmeats to go with it.

There were no presents wrapped in shiny paper, no cards or envelopes or words of congratulation. But I can't remember missing any of this.

I did receive presents, though I did not think of them that way. Along with a lot of knowledge. So much that it has taken years for me to unwrap it.

Afterwards, neither I nor anyone else delivered a speech. There were many things to say, but I for one could find no words, they had all drained out of me.

The other people present, who were all women, did have some words, which were far too soft and private to go into a speech.

They sat down and I sat down and after some time they asked me a few questions. My answers were unlikely to have been illuminating.

The only light I remember came from the lamps that were switched on as night fell and the women continued to speak among themselves, almost exclusively about a person who had been with me earlier but was unfortunately unable to join us afterwards.

⁂

That same person was growing increasingly familiar with the Bible, but there was certainly no mention of this during the allotted thirty minutes of my ceremony. In fact, no one officiated in the name of any religion, nor called upon the name of God. Strangely enough, though, religion had been invoked as the reason for the event to be held in the first place.

A few years earlier, I had been at a secular primary school where religion was nonetheless part of the syllabus. One of our school plays was about David and Goliath, and I was the prophet Samuel who held a horn and tipped some imaginary oil over David's head in the midst of his brethren. I was wearing my teacher's tatty, striped dressing-gown, there was a beard of white cotton-wool stuck to my chin, and all I had to say was 'With this horn of oil I anoint thee.'

Not long after that there was a clatter from the wings as Goliath emerged. 'Come to me,' he was supposed to roar in David's direction, 'and I will give thy flesh unto the fowls of the air, and to the beasts of the field.' Except that as he stepped onto the stage the audience burst out laughing, which might have been because he was so plump and pink, or due to the din of his hired armour which was like dishes being washed up in a hurry, so it couldn't have been easy to hear what he was saying.

Then David, swinging his sling, answered: 'Thou comest to me with a sword, and with a spear, and with a shield, but I come to thee in the name of the Lord of hosts, the God of the armies of Israel.'

With this he swung his sling one last time and Goliath began collapsing in slow motion, his noisy armour finally jutting out against the stage so that he could not actually lie down and die, leading to further mirth from the audience.

Our performance that evening was one reason why the story of David, and the smooth river-stone that sank into Goliath's forehead, remained freshly present for me. But then so did many of the other stories, because of their epic strangeness, the desert and the miracles, the boat full of animals floating on the floodwater, the man who walked out of a whale and the serpent that spoke.

As for the Lord, given all His heightened words and majestic powers, I decided round about the age of nine or ten to try and pray to Him.

Up until then, this was something I had only done at school. In the classroom at lunchtime, just before we brought out our sandwich boxes, we had to make sure our desks were clear, hold out our hands on one side and then the other for inspection, keeping the palms wide open to prove there was no red dust hidden in their creases from the marbles patch where we had been playing at break. Then we were all supposed to close our eyes and recite *For what we are about to receive may the Lord make us truly thankful. Amen.*

First thing in the morning in the school hall there had also been the Lord's Prayer, when all those in the whole school were supposed to close their eyes while starting off *Our Father which art in heaven.* If you cheated you could open your eyes a tiny bit in the middle and see everyone else's eyelids sealed and heads bowed, with words mumbling out of their mouths.

The Lord certainly was not mentioned at home, nor did it ever seem to be the right time to start asking questions about Him. Still, I did wonder about heaven, which was where He was supposed to be, because if you looked up on a clear day the sky seemed to go on forever with no particular place hidden inside it however far you could see.

I could not imagine Him or anyone else walking around on the clouds because they were always changing shape and drifting in and out of sight, while apparently the Lord was there all the time. Where did He go, for example, if He happened to be on one of those great swollen-bellied storm clouds that moved in over our street, brushed the day into darkness and finally burst, cracking our windowpanes with hailstones?

However, none of these considerations prevented me from wanting to try and pray. So before going to sleep at night I closed the door to my room, feeling vaguely guilty because praying was not what you did in our house. Sitting down on the mat next to the bed I dutifully pressed my palms together with the fingers pointing upwards, closed my eyes and began: *Our Father.* But the 'our' that had seemed right at school because there were so many of us praying did not feel altogether appropriate now that I was alone.

So I started again: *Dear Lord.* There followed a long silence because I had no idea of what I wanted to say. Besides which, 'Dear' was what you started a letter with, you never actually said it. I didn't, anyway. And then, when I eventually opened my eyes, I felt too close to the ground. So I got up onto the candlewick bedspread and started all over again.

I tried out various positions, at our house or Granny Lily's, starting with one sentence and then another. But the truth was that I needed to know whom I was speaking to, and more or less where that person might be. After all, why would the Lord be there just because I had decided to pray to him? Then again, how did other people know He was there if He was invisible in the first place, and, anyway, if He was invisible how come everyone said He had a beard?

I stopped trying to pray after a few weeks. But it did not seem right to simply go into my room, climb into bed and slip between the sheets. Was it the absence of any prayer, or the posture I had been in, or the moment of stillness that I needed? Whatever it was, in that space after I left the floor and before lying down, something seemed to be missing.

I did not see any adults praying, except for the teachers when everyone was saying the Lord's Prayer at school, though it was always difficult to tell if the teachers' mouths were actually moving, because they were standing quite far away and also because you weren't supposed to look in their direction since they might notice you with your eyes open. I might have asked Granny Lily or her sister Essie about all this, but somehow, as with everyone else, the question never came up.

Then one evening before nightfall, a man rang the doorbell at Granny Lily's house and stood waiting at the entrance. Granny Lily said something to Grandpa Joe, who gave her a grunt and told me to come with him.

We walked only as far as the house on the corner of the block opposite the park, which was in fact a shul. Grandpa Joe had a little velvet bag embroidered with silver that his tallith swished out of, and he also had a yarmulke like all the other men and his was black. He gave me one too.

There were men in jackets and ties and white shirts, there was the fresh smell of Grandpa Joe as I stood next to him, from the starch in his shirt and the jar of blue mud with which he washed his hands after working with electricity. Rays of clean vapour seemed to come out of him as he spoke to some of the other men along the wooden benches. It didn't seem difficult at all for him to find his words here, he just opened his mouth and they came out, and his smile flickered in the dim light.

Then everyone hushed.

There were men in front with yarmulkes and prayer shawls and beards, looking at everyone else including me so I had to pat my own yarmulke to make sure it had not slipped off my head. Everyone was saying prayers. They all knew what to say except for me and sometimes the words broke into a kind of song.

As the men spoke and sang their knees went rubbery, bending backwards and forwards as if they wanted to start walking except that there were benches in front of them and their feet were stuck to the floor. The whole place was swaying with their sloping bodies, including Grandpa Joe's which was among the shorter ones. I tried out the bending but it didn't feel right.

Then two men were opening a carved wooden cupboard and out came a double scroll wrapped in deep velvet that one of them walked with for a few steps, holding it against himself close as a baby before he unrolled it and read from it using words that I knew were in Hebrew.

There were more prayers and then a man had a ram's horn in his hand. It was twisted and shiny as ivory on the outside and dark as the inside of an ear.

He raised it to his lips and blew and the sound went upwards into the air and right through the ceiling. It was a cry and a call and a terrible complaint, a train in the night that only stopped where nobody could see it.

The men all around me weren't the same during a long moment. They had a streak of difference in their faces, what was it that had been woken in them with that sound?

Then it was all over, and the men were having quiet conversations with each other in their voices from before. They looked pleased if not relieved as they walked off into the evening just as I did with Grandpa Joe, though as soon as he left the others he wasn't speaking any more.

I was not invited to go again. But in the weeks after that I remembered what had happened, when passing the shul on the way to the park to fly my kite. I had made it myself, gumming bright triangular panels of tissue-paper over the balsa-wood rods of the frame, knotting the tail with cloth ribbons made by Granny Lily.

I managed to get the kite to skim over the short yellow grass and lift so as to miss anyone who happened to be walking past, then gain a bit of height and even fly for a few tail-spinning moments with its colours swirling. But then it drifted downwards with a will of its own that no amount of running across the grass and tugging at the string could counter, before it nose-dived, rustling and tearing, into the branches of the closest plane tree.

That was nothing like the sound of the ram's horn in the shul, rising with such wild and despairing ease through the ceiling to reach the sky.

Three

My thirteenth birthday ceremony took place about twenty-five centimetres from the ground.

A cushion of air below the feet might be thought of as a good preparation for take-off from puberty to the early stages of adulthood. In my case it was not exactly a cushion, my feet were resting on a solid surface and yet I was off the ground. This was appropriate when I come to think of it now, more particularly in connection with my mother.

As I have already said, I am the fruit of the union between a blessed one and a wild mountain goat. That is: my father, something of a mixed blessing when considered from a certain angle, and my mother, living on the steep slopes of her life, holding on wilfully and every now and then taking off, her wings always ready to stretch out from under her starched white coat.

I remember her speaking to my father one evening at supper about the day she had spent working as a doctor at Baragwanath Hospital, which was in the township of Soweto outside Johannesburg.

There was a group of women sitting outside in the

grass, she said. She had seen them at lunchtime, and not for the first time; they were still there when she left. *Just sitting there doing nothing*, she added, the word 'nothing' expelled from her mouth, sprung with a mixture of puzzlement and moral indignation.

I almost never saw my mother simply sitting somewhere doing nothing. She rarely sat at all, let alone on the grass, and even when she did sit, she still seemed to be striding inside herself. Unlike my father, who showed as little inclination to leave Johannesburg as a nail driven into a plank of wood, my mother would have been off and away at a moment's notice, in search of greener pastures. She did not admit to this until years later, though. She was not someone to speak much about herself and her desires.

She could become utterly distressed if she saw a tree being felled.

She could stand before a painting, drawn hypnotically into its framed world. In a childlike voice she would exclaim: *If only I could paint!*

She described her dreams as if she had just walked out of a cinema. But apart from their graphic precision and startling strangeness, she found almost no words to name her inner world.

Her days were filled with action, as air fills a balloon to its tense outer limits. Action in the here and now, with brief interludes such as those when she received letters from her parents. Then it was back to the all-encompassing present, with little thought for the past, let alone ancestry or tradition and its rituals.

Those of my parents' friends who were Jewish did not make much of such things either, ignoring all the designated high holidays and festivities. Instead, some of them had Christmas. So towards the end of December, during the summer holidays of the late 1950s, my parents and I (my brother and sister had not yet been born) would leave behind us the land-locked city of Johannesburg and head four hundred miles eastwards to the little village of Isipingo, near Durban, at the edge of the wild green sea, where some friends of my parents had their home.

It took us a full day and part of the night to get there, not only because of inevitable breakdowns to our little grey Morris Minor, but also because we always stopped on the way in the town of Estcourt to buy from the Farmer's Co-operative Bacon Factory a considerable round of ham, pink and moist and wrapped in a neat white fatty skin.

This was our contribution to the Isipingo Christmas feast, which continued for days on end and included turkey and ham and fish that Hari the Indian fisherman caught out on the rocks with hooks all the way down his line that could wind in six at a shot, all of them flashing as they wriggled for their lives.

There were little silver tickeys in the Christmas pudding among the raisins and rum so you had to watch out for your teeth, and doorfuls of visitors and the sound of the sea right in my bedroom, constantly licking with rough tongues at the walls.

No one mentioned the story of the bright star, the baby in the manger and the three wise kings. Instead, the men, amongst them my father, went into a huddle with a few of the women and spoke about politics, which meant working out who was bad and what to do about it. As in our home, you had to close the door so the conversation stayed in there. Cato Manor, I overheard them say as they came out. Sobukwe. Luthuli. Verwoerd.

Meanwhile several other women, amongst them my mother, went off to play Scrabble around a table in a side room. I was the one who passed around the bag of wooden letters clicking at the bottom of the bag, then watched them being composed into words and woven across the board. How rare to see my mother tranquilly occupying a chair and speaking in such warm tones with those other women as they all sipped at their tea and rearranged their letters, while the sea waltzed with sunlight at the window.

In the early evening my father would go walking along the beach. He could have been alone, far away in his thoughts, but I trailed after him and walked in his footsteps that were determined as spade-marks against the sea-sand.

I don't remember ever seeing my mother with a

spade. Her element was air. Which brings me back to the way my thirteenth birthday ceremony was suspended above the ground.

Not that my mother had anything at all to do with this. I doubt that she had been any more aware of the preparations for this moment than I was. But what exactly did those preparations consist of?

I imagine a low-ranking administrator in a khaki uniform, armed with a ballpoint pen and a trayful of official forms, doing the necessary paperwork in the rancid air of an obscure office. Above his desk, there would have been a framed photograph of Prime Minister Doctor Verwoerd, giving one of his maddeningly smug smiles to a scantily dressed, pouting girl from a Pirelli Tyre calendar on the opposite wall. I imagine him stabbing with a rubber stamp at a purple inkpad to finalise arrangements.

It might have been useful on the day of my thirteenth birthday for my mother to drive me to the place where I needed to be. Fortunately though, she did not yet have her licence. When she did start driving, the experience of being in the car with her was so nerve-wracking that I preferred to set out on foot if the destination was nearby.

Anyway, this question did not arise on the day in question in 1964.

I should add that we did not go to Isipingo that year. By then one of the adults who had come there for Christmas had committed suicide, after falling in love with our hostess. A number of the others were divorced, or had left the country to go into exile, or both.

☙

The year 1960 began in an exhausting way for my mother. Towards the end of March, after the Sharpeville massacre, our house began filling up with even more people than before, needing to say things to each other in private. They came, that is, if my father was there at all, because sometimes he said he was going out for a walk at night but did not return for a day or two.

Meanwhile my mother drifted pale as chalk down the passage, estranged from what was going on and ready for bed. She needed to be up very early the next morning to get to work. And then there was my little brother Allen, not yet one year old, breaking into her sleep with his wailing.

By the middle of the year she was definitely ready for a holiday, and found herself in an aeroplane for the first time, along with Allen and me, all of us going down through the clouds to Lod airport in the land of Israel.

And thus it was that at the age of almost nine years old I met the other half of my family. There was my uncle Jacky driving us out of the airport in an army jeep through what felt like the steam of a hot bath. He was smiling so that all his gums showed while my grandmother Toba stood at the back of the jeep and would not sit down, proud as a flagpole with the wind in her high-combed hair and brown eyes flecked with green looking out far away from the beauty of her face.

We went driving past blue gum trees with bark hanging like ancient skin from their trunks, sprinklers sowing jewels of water over and over across wide green fields; then it was breakfast time at my grandparents' house and there were salads sweet with tomatoes, olives big as eyes, fried eggs without bacon and stewed quinces spooned from jars of amber light.

There was my new grandfather Zalman with bushy eyebrows and sandpaper cheeks and my new aunt Tchya with the soft, shy smile that easily broke into laughter; everyone was laughing, even my mother in the company of this family she had been so far away from for more than ten years. They, too, had been in South Africa and now here they were in the land of Israel with turkeys gobbling in the yard and dimpled custard apples ripening on a lean tree and a road of fine, pale sand running outside the house.

At the bottom of the road there was an orange orchard, and beyond that the house of my Uncle Jacky and Aunt Ofra of the caring voice and sad love in her eyes, and my young cousins. And a monkey chained to a tree in the garden that could store grapes in its cheek for hours without biting into them.

Israel was a ride on blue Egged buses with my mother and Tchya, who knew where we needed to go. There were big women knitting in seats all around us, sugary songs blaring from the intercom and the bus driver driving as if he was in a bulldozer making the road; soldiers outside the windows crammed into jeeps and the backs of trucks, more soldiers hitchhiking and everyone stopping to give them a lift.

The bus stations were thick with an oily fog of diesel fumes through which all manner of travellers moved hectically with their hats and guns and holy books and grocery bags while all around them hawkers cried out their wares: newspapers, lemonade, falafel, cornets of salted sunflower and pumpkin seeds, and peeled, slippery prickly pears on slabs of ice.

At the bottom end of the country in Eilat the sun was white stinging hot, and, at the high end, Lake Kineret was a mirror that rippled when you entered it. In the middle, where the borders of the country were so close you could almost fasten a belt around them, soldiers lay hidden with binoculars in the grass.

In Tabgha and Caeseria and Ashkelon the Romans had gone away and left mosaics and columns and broken pots behind them. In Jerusalem there was a whole city inside the city like a baby in a woman's belly, and on the winding road not far away cars stood rusting among the pine trees: blasted skeletons of cars with no windows or wheels, yet still driving resolutely through the war they had not survived.

Nothing was finished in this place, you just had to turn around and something else would happen, it was like the moment when Tchya's boyfriend Izzy told me to look at the bird outside the window and when I glanced back he was giving her a kiss.

By the end of our stay I still did not know my mother very well but at least we had been on a journey together. Her family was mine too. And as for Israel, it was somehow a part of us even if we were not really a part of it.

So many people were Jewish in Israel that that wasn't even a question, and I was Jewish but apparently there was nothing I had to do about it since it was just how things were.

No one spoke about being Jewish in my mother's family, not because it was a secret but because it was so obvious. The only time they mentioned it was when they saw women in long sleeves with wigs, boys and men wrapped up in black with tassels and curls of hair hanging out like the tendrils of a plant with nothing to climb onto. They looked as if they were living somewhere else, in a country without a sun even if they were sweating.

They were apparently too Jewish.

But back in South Africa, when I was with Jewish friends it seemed that I was not Jewish enough, because unlike my family they were always doing something about it, like not eating bacon, or going to shul.

I did not know what to do about it.

I had half a family in Israel, but that wasn't any help.

Nothing seemed to be of any help.

⮧

By the end of 1962 I was none the wiser.

I was approaching the age of thirteen, and could already have been preparing for my bar mitzvah. But a bar mitzvah seemed to be out of the question, so I was not thinking about it.

We happened to be back in Israel, at my grand-parents' house: my mother, my brother and I, along with my father. Not that he particularly wanted to be there, this was just a stopover at his in-laws, probably to placate my mother. He would soon be spending a year in a physics laboratory in England, and we would be accompanying him.

While in Israel, he spent as little time at my grandparents' house as possible, often travelling off early to catch a bus so that he could discuss politics with a man in Be'er Sheva. But one morning he said he wanted to go for a walk so that he could speak to me.

Usually, if there was something on his mind then he would simply say it, we spoke often enough. I felt entirely at ease in his company unless he was angry, I could not bear it when he grew angry. So what could be of such great importance that he wanted us to go off somewhere else in order to talk about it?

I followed him in silence across the cool tiles of the entrance hall, through the screen door, over the polished concrete slabs of the veranda and out into the burning light of day.

Downhill, then, hot loose sand of the road slipping into my sandals. From a field of weeds, the voice of a donkey like the screeching of brakes. A bougainvillea bush against a wall, sunlight igniting its papery flowers. Machinery rusting in a shack at the bottom of the road.

We reached the shade of the orange orchard and made for the thick of it, my father bending to avoid the branches of trees laden with fruit. Then he finally came to a standstill and, quite abruptly, began speaking.

Some of my friends would already be preparing for their bar mitzvahs, he said. But he did not want me to have one.

I was immediately relieved. Not about the bar mitzvah – what did I care about such things right then – but about having done nothing wrong. My father was not going to get angry with me.

He'd had a bar mitzvah, he was saying, but it made no sense to him. The lessons had been deadly dull. He had learned the Hebrew words he needed to read out during the ceremony but did not have the faintest idea what they meant and simply recited them by rote. The whole event had been so sterile, he did not want me to go through the same ordeal.

My father usually spoke to me in measured tones, his head up in a cloud of pipe-smoke which was rough and sweet like burned rose petals. But he did not have his pipe that morning, and he was unusually hesitant and ill at ease. He did turn out to be angry, but not with me. His mood began to simmer like water in a pot with the lid clattering, and he repeated the word 'sterile' several times over.

I had never up until then heard him talking about his boyhood, and I imagined a scaled-down version of himself just as he was, with his moustache and bald spot, still wearing his grey flannel trousers and special shoes to make room for his gout, though I knew he hadn't had gout as a boy. I saw him sitting at a desk in Granny Lily's house, bent over a book, trying to concentrate on what he had to learn for his bar mitzvah, getting up, walking around in a creaky circle, sitting down again.

Just down the passageway from his room, at the front door: the grandfather clock, its brass pendulum permanently skewed to one side. Through the living room window, Grandpa Joe's lustreless grey electricity van stuck against the driveway.

I saw the suit Granny Lily had bought me; my friends running across our school soccer field, their heads full of Hebrew.

I saw Granny Lily smiling for me like a lamp in her home and the wrinkled horizons of trouble across her forehead.

I'd had no idea that my thirteenth birthday was of the least significance to my father, yet here he was saying I shouldn't have one, which seemed to mean, all of a sudden, that I possibly could have one after all.

If I said something.

My father was giving me a choice but at the same time he wasn't: I could not imagine doing anything he so badly did not want me to do. I was in thrall of him, there was no one I wanted to please more.

Besides, we were going to be away in England for the year and the bar mitzvah seemed to belong to the world of Johannesburg which we were leaving behind, weren't we, so what else was there to say? I would just drop the whole question back into an obscure box labelled BEING JEWISH, where it could sink down quietly and be forgotten.

By the time my father stopped talking I still had not opened my mouth to respond to him one way or another, out of a mixture of wonder that the matter of a bar mitzvah had been raised in the first place, uncertainty about the source of my father's turbulence, and, above all, fear that saying even a single word might disturb him even further.

On the way back towards my grandparents' house I was still bound up in my own muteness. What was this place inside myself where I lost my ability to speak?

Why, for once, had my father's wilfulness been torn through with such sharp emotion?

Had he perhaps been waiting for me to interrupt him? Not in order to go on trying to convince me, but simply so as to discover whom this son of his really was?

Even as we left, questions continued to arch over me like the trees in the orange orchard, their branches criss-crossing against the sky. We had stood together amongst them and my father had said what he wanted to say, but I had not answered him and, besides, there was something neither he nor I had spoken of at all.

It remained suspended like the oranges among the glossy dark leaves, a fruit we could not slice open since it was sealed as a secret and had to do with Jewishness. Whatever my father knew about it he would not share, and whatever I thought I knew I could not ask for more. What I almost knew was that raising this subject at all would have been like touching a very swollen sore.

So on that morning my father left his knowledge and I left my questions behind in the shadows of an orchard at the end of a hot sand road, a few hundred paces from my mother's parents' home in the land of Israel.

⁀

That event in the orchard occurred when we were all on our way to England at the end of 1962. And one year later, at the end of 1963, England was where I was determined to stay.

Not that anyone in my family found the country particularly hospitable. My father had problems setting up the laboratory at Reading University for which he had received a grant, and did not get on with the staff. One night, in the winter of the 'Big Freeze', he found himself upside-down in his car after skidding on ice, and came home badly shaken.

My mother could not at first find a job as a doctor. My little brother had difficulty making friends, one had to get permission from parents for children to see each other, it was like an administrative procedure. And as for my sister, who was born that year, she spent her first weeks in an incubator, though that was hardly the fault of the local inhabitants.

Meanwhile, I went to school in a bus in the early-morning obscurity, which had descended again before I came home, as if the days were nothing but a lean slice of light slipped into a sandwich of darkness.

The boys and girls in my class spoke English, and I thought that was the language I spoke too, except that the meaning of what they said to each other kept escaping me and I could neither decipher the code of their cliques nor locate the source of their laughter. I would have liked to join a school soccer team but there wasn't one, and though I did not like swimming I hardly understood why the school had a pool at all, since it was nothing but the muddy home to a teeming family of newts.

But nothing at school, not even the x in algebra or the finer details of the Battle of Thermopylae, was as problematic as something I slowly and dimly became aware of, especially towards the end of 1963.

Christmas was approaching and we drove through the rain and fog visiting one South African political exile after another. Some were living in shadows and discomfort, others were snug in their new homes, but none of them had really left South Africa.

They had yellow grass mats on the floor with the smell of the veld plaited into them; fat pots of smoked red clay, masks pulling stiff ritual faces on the walls, the latest novels by Nadine Gordimer and Doris Lessing on a coffee table side by side with *The Spy Who Came in From the Cold* and *The Sailor Who Fell from Grace with the Sea.*

They played Miriam Makeba songs on their gramophones. *Where did that naughty little flea go?* she sang in her slinky voice and they laughed knowingly and sipped at whisky swirling in ice, though my parents would not touch the stuff. Then they started speaking about politics again.

I knew that this was about the country they had escaped from and wanted to go back to. And I understood that they could not return, whatever the tide that was tugging the underbelly of their lives back there. It would be far too dangerous.

But what did that mean?

What exactly did I glean, from which stray words, which glances?

One evening at home in Reading we were watching the evening news on television. There were two men, broadly smiling. I did not know them, but their faces and accents were of a kind that was familiar to me: they could have been friends of my parents. And they had just escaped from a prison in Johannesburg, disguised as priests.

But what had such people been doing in prison in the first place?

In Johannesburg?

Once again I knew this had to do with politics. And politics, it seemed, meant playing with fire, even if you could come away apparently unscathed and smiling with relief.

Not very long afterwards, we started preparing to return to South Africa. For the first time in my life I found myself not wanting to accept what my father took for granted: as far as he was concerned we were going back and that was that, whatever danger he might have been aware of.

I'm staying, I declared quietly at the end of the year, looking hopelessly around our inadequate flat with half our possessions already in boxes and the rest waiting to be packed.

Please, I said, more loudly.

Then, bursting out so that the moment smelled like a fuse box after the lights had gone out, *We're all going to stay.*

But what chance did the tears of a twelve-year-old have of outweighing the insistent, long-distance, sweet-as-blood siren-call of the Struggle?

Four

It was the beginning of 1964 and I was at the local all-boys high school in Johannesburg. I had skipped a class on returning from England because of everything I had apparently learned there. But a lot of what I needed to know now I had *not* learned there, so I was working quite hard to catch up with the others in my class.

For a start, there was the Afrikaans language. How could a whole language have slipped my mind while I was in England? I sat in the Afrikaans class squinting at the word ''n' in a book, asking myself how it could be a translation of the indefinite article 'a'. What were the meanings of all the other words in the sentences that made up paragraphs of the story I was supposed to have read the night before, and how was it possible that in the space of a year in England I had almost turned into a foreigner?

I had untanned skin, a full year virtually without playing any sport, and an English accent I did not even know I had picked up but now wanted to get rid of because I was being mocked for it at school. What

I needed was to blend into the scenery, which meant becoming South African again.

Well, at least I could play rugby.

Rugby was what you played at my high school if you wanted to be like everyone else and maybe even better, by eventually getting into one of the photos of well-groomed, solemnly smiling, square-shouldered players in the top rugby teams going back decades and lining the walls of the school hall.

A rugby field was where you could run and sweat, get into a raw crush of other boys and then run some more, even if you didn't actually manage to touch the ball. For four, six, eight hours a week or more, straight after the last class, that is what I religiously did. And with dollops of willpower and just a pinch of skill, I ended up as hooker of the under-thirteen A-team, my arms around the thick necks of two tank-like boys at the heart of the grinding scrum.

In the evenings I went jogging with a friend, under the plane trees and street lamps, alongside hedges and the rich creosote stink of split-pole fences, past dogs that came battering and slavering at every gate. Step by step, breath by rusty, heaving breath I ran into the darkness, beating with rubber soles at the grass and flagstones and tarred suburban streets, working England out of my system, letting Johannesburg back in.

In mid-July of that same year, 1964, during the school's winter holidays, something very different happened: I found myself travelling to Durban, four hundred miles east of Johannesburg on the coast. It was just over a month before my thirteenth birthday, and I was to stay at the home of a rabbi.

This particular aspect of the trip was not due to any intention of my own, nor had my parents had anything to do with it. Call it fate, or accident, or the winds of chance that carried me into the rabbi's home.

I did not know him, and it was nothing less than an embarrassment to me to find myself being driven from the main Durban station to the rabbi's door.

This was after a train ride with a group of boys from my school. We were members of the school choir. We had been entered into the Johannesburg Eisteddfod, and – I think to the amazement of us all – had been awarded first prize.

Our music teacher was the one most deserving of a prize, though. Not only for coaxing a bunch of boys rustling with the early onset of testosterone into joining a choir and training for hours on end, but above all for surviving in that high school in the first place.

Our Thursday mornings, for example, were given

over to 'cadets': boys in military khaki marching around for hours in platoons like toy soldiers with no minds of their own, swinging left and right, saluting and occasionally fainting in the heat while bigger boys barked hoarsely in their ears. That activity was given prime importance by the powers that be. Who cared if any of us could sing?

Our music teacher's name was Bird, Mr Michael Bird, and he had a certain touch of innocence that went with his widely stretched smile, his undaunted ardour and his name.

He was also able to move both ears simultaneously in alarmingly large circles to either side of his balding head while the muscles of his face appeared to remain motionless; this, he told us, would improve our singing immensely.

But what was such information worth, compared to the much-fingered photographs that were being surreptitiously passed around the class? How was it possible for a man and three women to be doing anything like that together? With nothing on at all, the stiff lines and soft and hairy places of their bodies so close to each other? In broad daylight?

Well, next thing, those of us who had volunteered for the choir were singing 'Summer is icumen in' in dovetailing four-part harmony, not the thirteenth-century Middle English version of the song but a slightly modified one:

Summer is a-coming in
Loudly sing cuckoo
Groweth seed and bloweth mead
and springs the wood anew
Sing cuckoo!

Ewe bleateth after lamb,
Calf loweth after cow,
Bullock starteth, buck verteth,
Merry sing cuckoo!
Cuckoo, cuckoo!
Well singest thou cuckoo,
Nor cease thou never now!
Sing cuckoo, Sing cuckoo!

We were entirely ignorant of the sneaking suspicion, only voiced by an academic years later, that the use of the earthy word 'verteth' (meaning 'to fart') and the mention of the cuckoo (known for its predatory habits but hardly for the quality of its song) might point to this actually being a song composed by philandering, adulterous monks, warning twelfth-century husbands to look out for their possibly errant wives.

But there was Mr Bird, no wiser than we were, perched in the bright tree of his enthusiasm, urging us on. And there he was a few months later, vaulting over the plush velvet chairs at the City Hall in order to congratulate us on winning the Eisteddfod.

As a result, we would all be going off to Durban

to sing our song at the International Arts League of Youth meeting that July.

Strange, because my father was also going. To present a paper at a conference about teaching physics, he told me. And, again by coincidence, someone else would be there: my Great-Aunt Essie, staying that very winter at a beachfront hotel. We could have lunch together, she suggested before leaving.

Twelve years old, almost thirteen, and for the first time I would be off on holiday and neither travelling with my family nor staying with them. Going away on my own business, meeting up with my father man to man and seeing my great-aunt on the side.

Winter was a-coming in, time to sing a deceptive song.

⁓

There were forms to fill in before taking the train to Durban, and one line concerned my religion.

Jewish, of course. It couldn't be anything else, could it? Jewish, not simply by a process of elimination, nor because the notion had much apparent substance for me, but there it was, 'Jewish', with my tick in a box beside it.

I learned I would be staying with a rabbi and his family, and soon after my arrival in the city there was the rabbi's wife, opening the door to me.

That evening I sat at the rabbi's dinner table, opposite the rabbi's son, who had just had his bar mitzvah. It was inevitable that the rabbi should ask me about mine.

Back in Johannesburg, before I'd set off for Durban, my parents had agreed that it was perfectly natural for a Jewish boy to be allotted a Jewish family to stay with. But who would have dreamed, asked my mother, that I would end up staying with a rabbi?

A rabbi? added my father, his sarcasm peppered with disbelief, then salted with laughter. *When you were born your mother and I decided that you could become anything you wanted, except for a rabbi.* And now it was a rabbi whose quiet question came hovering with great wings over the dinner table.

I sat sinking into the soles of my shoes, with no ally to turn to because this was a question for me alone, and already the answer was in my downcast eyes and the heat that rose up into my face.

Even the invisible thought that I *should* be having a bar mitzvah, decreed at some obscure time by an unknown, fierce-eyed ancestor now advancing insistently through the undergrowth of my mind, must surely be apparent to the rabbi.

The rabbi's wife looked at me with what I thought might be pity.

The rabbi's son looked at me with what I suspected to be disdain, though I could not be sure, because to my surprise, once I had answered the truth as economically as possible, they neither cross-examined me nor shunned me, in fact did not slight me in any way. Instead, they changed the subject. They might have been embarrassed for me, but their manner towards me did not appear to change in any way: I was their guest, not their hostage.

I have no memory of what I had for lunch with my Great-Aunt Essie at her beachfront hotel not long afterwards. The meal was most likely served upon one of those white tablecloths starched and ironed till it glowed almost silver, by a waiter wearing an imperial sash across his equally starched white livery.

Nor can I remember what we spoke about; we probably mentioned my father, who was the apple of my great-aunt's eye and whom I had seen the day before. We had gone out together to see a film in the middle of Durban.

I have no memory of how I reached the hotel, or what it looked like. I do not remember the sea that day, only the sand at the hotel end of the beach, which was full of dips as if it had been dug up by a multitude of little spades and then forgotten. Also, there was a kiosk in the sand with no one in it because it was winter, but even if winter was the season and the wind was blowing, that still did not explain why I was standing there shivering uncontrollably.

At which point did we go outside after lunch, and where had my great-aunt found the newspaper she was now holding a bit closer? She indicated to me a headline on the front page about a lecturer from the University of the Witwatersrand who had been arrested on the road out of Durban, and the man in question was apparently a Mr Baruch Hirson.

That was my father's name but it could not have been my father, of course, because he had told me, less than twenty-four hours earlier, that he would see me back in Johannesburg in just a few days' time. And since my father's words held greater weight for me than those printed black on white in the newspaper, it stood to reason that when I returned home my father would be there.

However, just a glance at my great-aunt Essie's face told me that this would not be the case. Her features revealed precisely what my suddenly opaque spirit would not admit, though the knowledge had already penetrated my mind as I stood there with her, facing the pitted stretch of beach sand.

My mind was being laid out horizontally in my head and anaesthetised, as when I'd had a hernia operation a few years earlier. *Blow into the orange balloon*, the doctor had said, and then slowly I went sinking down, watching the world around me melt at the edges and turn to vapour. Except that I was not lying down now and my eyes remained open as I fixed them on the sand and the shadowy dips and the desolate café.

Let's go back in, said my great-aunt.

But there was nowhere at all that I wanted to go.

⌒

Once all the boys from the choir were settled into their green leather compartments on the train going home, some of them started speaking about girls; one in particular displayed extravagant but unlikely knowledge of a girl's intimate parts.

When we stopped at a station, a man came to tap the wheels of the train with a long-handled hammer, checking by the sound they made that they were not cracked; several boys made jokes about him, nicknaming him a 'tapologist'. Then some of them fought, and others read war comics. There seemed no end to the journey.

I tried to strike up a conversation with a boy a few years older than I was who had a quiet way of listening; we had already spoken a few times though we were not friends. But I soon realised that speaking to anyone from my school would not get me very far if my opening gambit was to be something like *You know what? My father has just been arrested...*

I was dropped outside our house in Johannesburg.

It was cold.

The grass and shrubs and arching leaves of agapanthi in the garden seemed almost grey in the cloudy light.

My mother opened the door.

We did not hug or touch at all.

She went to sit on the Morris settee to the side of the bay window and wanted to speak to me. I sat down reluctantly on the settee next to her though I had wanted to retreat to my room. I had lived all my life under the same roof as my mother yet to me she felt like a stranger.

She started telling me how the police had searched the house, and concluded that the buttons they had found fixed to walls in the bedrooms were linked to some secret underground communication system. In fact, they were wired up to a bell in the maid's room out in the garden, installed there by the previous occupants in order to call on her at any hour of the day or night.

I did not want to listen to all this.

I did not want to hear her speaking at all, nor was it much comfort to think of the privacy of our house being invaded by the police.

We sat there at arm's length on the settee and

silence fell between us, filled with my father's absence. We had no idea how to speak to each other, not even to ask how the other was feeling.

I looked around the room. Everything was stuck in place like ice against ice: the fire-grate and copper bin of split pine logs, woven grass mat, shelves with double rows of books up to the moulded ceiling, my father's varnished yellow pine desk and his tobacco jar to the side of the gramophone loudspeaker, a brass pestle in a brass mortar holding back the door to the passage, my mother's hand finally in my hand, stiff with cold.

⁂

Where was my brother on that day when I returned from Durban? At nursery school? Not yet awake? My sister was probably sleeping. She was nine months old.

Soon afterwards I went with my mother to a party at my brother's nursery school. I stood to one side along with my mother and a number of other parents as everyone started singing:

One little elephant balancing,
step by step on a piece of string.
He thought it such a jolly stunt

that he called up another little elephant.
Two little elephants balancing...

A first child went around the large room in a circle, arms stretched wide, dipping to the left and to the right, balancing on the ground, then called up a second one. Soon all the children were occupying the room, arms out, singing the song.

My mother and I were also balancing on a piece of string, one end tied to our house and the other to a prison called the Old Fort in the middle of Johannesburg, where my father was being detained.

My mother visited him there but I was not allowed to. According to the regulations, children could not enter a prison. They had to wait until they turned sixteen.

Five

On 25 August 1964, my thirteenth birthday, I woke up as usual before 7am.

I dressed in a clean white shirt and grey flannel trousers, tied the laces of my black shoes, knotted my red-and-black-striped tie and smoothed down my collar. I had a breakfast of Jungle Oats, a fried egg on a toasted slice of brown bread and a mug of hot Milo.

Before going out I slipped on my jacket, which was black and had an image of a red lion stitched against the breast pocket. The lion was raised up on its hind legs, knees flexed, erect tail almost brushing the back of its mane. In one paw it held aloft a green laurel wreath, and its tongue came flickering out of its mouth like a flame. Below it, inscribed in capital letters across a curved white scroll, was the word ARISE.

Hitching my khaki canvas schoolbag over a shoulder, I left the house and went walking up the hill to high school, under plane trees hung with weavers' nests, past bus stops and lampposts, perfectly waxed cars jammed one behind the other, maroon shale in raw layers where the hillside had been cut away, mansions perched over the city, obscured by high stone walls and thick foliage.

Other boys wearing the same uniform came funnelling towards the school entrance on foot, on bicycles and in cars, some older boys revving their motorbikes as they rode past, then standing for as long as possible at the shed where they had parked them, helmets tucked under their arms as they engaged in manly discussion.

At school assembly there was a hushed shuffling as the head boy called out *School, rise!* The headmaster and a few other teachers came onto the stage and, upon being told to, everyone gave collective voice in a slow songless chant to the words of the Lord's Prayer: *Our Father which art in heaven, Hallowed be thy name. Thy kingdom come, thy will be done.*

One of the teachers announced some sports results. We filed out. Classes began. There was a break, followed by a second, longer one for lunch, then more classes, but I packed up my books and left before the last one ended, walking out past the brick walls of the school's west wing.

As far as I was aware none of the other boys knew where I was going. My mother had written a note to excuse me and I was not asked any questions. Along the corridors, I heard voices filtering from one classroom after another: teachers speaking, a boy responding to a question, half a phrase in Afrikaans.

I crossed the patio to reach the gate giving onto the street. When school ended there was usually a crowd, but now the dry crunching of gravel came only from under the soles of my own shoes.

My mother was in a car waiting for me outside the high school. Not yet able to drive, she was sitting next to a friend who could do so and had taken off work that afternoon.

We did not speak while travelling around the school and its sports fields, alongside the trees of Empire Avenue to Clarendon Circle, past the box-houses of policemen and their parched, rectangular gardens; then uphill, not much more than a five-minute journey though every second stretched out with the eagerness of a spring being released inside me, at the same time contracting, coil upon coil, with anxiety.

Our Father which art. Thy kingdom. And lead us. Not.

It was two o'clock in the afternoon.

The car had stopped at a spot on the hill overlooking our high school, almost equidistant between our house to the north, and the suburb to the north-west where my grandparents lived.

Above us, the ramparts of the prison known as the Old Fort, planted with a row of giant cacti, the long-thorned blades of their leaves slashing against the sky.

Below us, about a dozen paces downslope across the tar apron of the prison parking lot, an ice-blue Volkswagen Beetle.

I got out alone and walked towards it.

My father was sitting inside.

Of course that was my father, but with a smile on his face that was not a smile, sitting but not as he usually sat, in a manner that was crumpled and in a place that was not his. Since when did he occupy the back seat of a car? Here was a policeman getting out to let me, too, into the back, then returning to the driver's seat next to a second policeman.

Both of them were young men wearing slate-coloured safari-suit uniforms with short-sleeved shirts and matching short trousers baring their muscular, hairy thighs. The one in the passenger seat had an aluminium comb sticking out of one long sock, though it could not have been of much use to him because his head, like his partner's, had been shorn close to the scalp.

It was a 'special visit', one my father himself had applied for, claiming that as a Jewish father he needed to be present on his son's thirteenth birthday.

There were no photographs, no gifts of any tangible kind; no singing or elevating sound; no holy words, not even my father's first name since no one spoke it out loud.

The last time we had seen each other was six weeks earlier, in Durban. *I'll see you back in Johannesburg in just a few days' time*, my father had said.

How long ago had that been? His absence had blurred my notion of time, I had not counted the days. But what did I care, he was there now, right next to me. I glanced into his eyes and saw how sadness diluted the strength of his gaze, wariness weighing against his pride.

We held onto each other's hands. I felt the heat of his palm and the pulsing grip of his gout-jammed fingers as, in answer to his questions, I gave him news of the family, telling him how my mother was, what my brother and sister were doing. But since when did I give my father news of his own family? I was not speaking to an overseas friend of his on the telephone. Since when did I tell him about such things?

Then again, what else was there to speak about? My sentences were punched through with holes of silence, my father's were not much better. The quantity of pent-up feeling I had to share with him was in inverse proportion to the number of words I was able to find, each one of them attached to a shadow and each shadow saturated with the need to be with him but not like this, not to be speaking to him in this way, not to be held hostage alongside him, witnessing him in all his helplessness.

I had already guessed in the previous weeks that he

would most likely be absent for longer than I wanted to think about. The solemn, powdered features of my great-aunt's face and the deep furrow of her brow had told me so in Durban, as had my mother's sleepless face in Johannesburg.

There had been news in the papers of other arrests followed by court cases and prison sentences. There had been all those South Africans in England, and the word 'exile', which for me had come to mean 'so-very-happy-to-have-got-out-in-the-nick-of-time-even-if-I-badly-want-to-go-back-now'. Which in turn meant that if you happened to be in South Africa and did not get out quickly enough, your fate could easily be sealed for you by people who definitely did not have your own welfare at heart.

Minions of those very people were sitting right there in the front seats of the Volkswagen, the backs of their heads seemingly as sensitive as a pair of bottle-brushes to what was going on behind them.

My father sat in his corner of the back seat and I sat next to him, our hands sunk together. Well before time was up we had run out of words to say. Everything between us was cooped up in the present, and yet slowly the moments proceeded, following unstoppably upon each other like a slow leak over which neither of us had any control.

Then suddenly one of the policemen announced the end, in either English or Afrikaans; just a single blunt sentence or a sawn-off phrase. I was in no state to pay much attention to the exact words he used.

So it was all over.

Had that been thirty minutes?

No doubt not a second longer, just as had been agreed on well in advance.

☙

Across the road from the Old Fort, set in the flagstones of the pavement, lay an air-vent linked to the adjoining residence for nurses. Later, I passed the place once in a while and watched the pale bellyfuls of steam barely whispering as they emerged, warped and wavering, through the vent's iron grid.

But I doubt that I even glanced in that direction as I left my father behind and went off, accompanied by my mother and her friend, to have tea at the nearby flat of someone they both knew.

I remember only how separate I felt, and how everyone else seemed like a stranger, even in the living room I entered, all quietness and tasteful paintings, carpets and filtered light, before the lamps were switched on at nightfall. At one end there was a table laid out with a spread of hot and cold drinks, club sandwiches and sweetmeats.

Perhaps I had a smile like the one I'd seen stuck on the face of a motorcyclist after being knocked off his bike by a car. He spun through the air and landed on his helmet in the middle of the road, then got up holding that smile hard against his teeth as if nothing had happened.

It had.

So much had happened to me that there was nothing left over now.

I sat down and shuttered myself up, barely heard the women speaking near me, would not taste the carefully prepared spread but wanted only the heat of tea going down my throat and into the darkness of my body.

And though I kept thinking of my father, in my thoughts I refused to follow him in the Volkswagen beyond the bolted frontier of the prison's outer door, fought against conceiving of him in a prison cell at all.

His presence in prison was no more substantial to me than the steam coming out of the underworld of that vent just across the road. But even if I tried to shut out thoughts of him confined in a cell it was too late, because part of me had gone in there with him.

In this way, on the afternoon of my thirteenth birthday I was not only separated from my father but also divided from something of myself, since there was already an unnamed, unvisited, unwanted prison cell inside me.

At primary school, several years earlier, something had happened that stuck in my mind: at the end of the morning, the secretary's voice came over the intercom above the blackboard asking a boy in our class and that boy's two brothers to pack their bags and go to the secretary's office.

What could that be about?

All three brothers?

The oldest was quiet and unassuming, he had freckles under a mop of coppery red hair and was the best swimmer in our class. In the following weeks I went to visit him in a big house just up the road from where we lived. His father had died, and everything was being packed away so that the family could move elsewhere. The three brothers walked around the desolate rooms, their steps echoing as their world disappeared into cardboard boxes.

But this was not what had happened to me, was it? I was not about to move from our house and my father had not died, he simply wasn't there, his presence suspended up in the Old Fort, which was cut into the ridge of the city and almost visible from the high school I attended day after day.

I would be in class trying to conjugate a French irregular verb, or waiting in the queue at the tuck-shop to buy a Cornish pasty for lunch, or out in the long sun-laden afternoon, sweating my way across one of the rugby fields which lined the southern side of our school, while my father sat locked up in the Old Fort hardly fifteen minutes from there on foot.

Yet it was not possible to believe that the two of us were living in the same city, on the same day.

Why did he seem even further away now that we had seen each other? His absence surrounded me, as palpable as it was unreal.

In our mathematics class, the teacher taught us about infinity: if you have a bag of marbles and you want to take out ten of them, one by one, how many times must you put your hand in the bag?

Ten times.

But if you want to take out no marbles, how many times must you put your hand in the bag?

An infinite number.

I remembered how that teacher's pale and leathery palm had closed and opened with nothing in it.

The days and weeks went by, and slowly I began my apprenticeship of loss, simultaneously trying to seal the lesson from myself, just as termites apply themselves to repairing the mound of their nest when it has been kicked over. On frenetic legs, with grain after sand-grain of blind perseverance, they hopelessly seek to reconstitute the world as it had been before.

Something started happening to me at night, after supper.

My mother would be in her bedroom, just the other side of my wall, working her way towards another medical exam, journals and tomes spread across her square wooden table, a bowl of nuts and dried fruit to one side that she pecked at from time to time. My brother and sister were asleep in their bedroom across the passage.

I would have done my homework but had no wish to read, or lie down, or do anything at all.

My door would be closed.

I walked the few paces between the walls, or leaned against a bookcase, or sat down on a chair; the light was on or off, and my eyes were open or closed, it made no difference, because now was the time that darkness came from nowhere and found me out. It began filling the space before me, reaching into greater darkness, soundlessly, motionlessly yet still accumulating all around me, deepening further than any well. The thought came to me that this darkness was death, and that after death there would be nothing at all left of myself in the world.

And my father was gone.

It was as if his absence had unplugged the darkness inside me, and now it would not stop pouring out until it swallowed me entirely.

I would start crying, but without making a sound. There was no one I wanted to turn to. The one other person awake in the house, my mother, was no one to me.

Then, eventually, caught up in exhaustion, I went to sleep.

For how many weeks, or months, or more, did this go on? I no longer know. I did not allow myself to think about what was happening. It was one more secret, and I tried to keep it even from myself. But once the idea of death had been planted deep inside me, it went on growing. And even when the nightly spells of darkness diminished and then did not recur, I could still look inwards at any time and see my own death growing there, just as one sees a tree on the near horizon at twilight, the outline of its trunk and branches gradually being taken by the night.

At school I retreated into a trench of my own making, ready to raise my arms and stand by whatever my father had done, though I did not yet have a clear idea of what exactly that might be.

At least some of the other boys must have known he was in prison for political reasons, but would not speak of this directly. Instead, they came up to me at break and, lacing their words with poison, asked: *If a kaffir went into your house and killed your father and raped your mother and your sister* then *what would you do, hey?*

And though the boys were each different their

words were virtually the same, as if they had concocted them together.

Were we all living in a place so narrow that only a single question could be asked there, while the one expected answer was fitted with the trigger of a gun?

⌒

My father was held at the Old Fort for just under ninety days while awaiting trial, for the most part in solitary confinement. He later wrote about this experience, describing how he delivered physics lectures to his empty cell for the first weeks but could not continue without demonstration equipment or the possibility of writing out equations.

Then, as a special favour, he managed to obtain a pencil stub from the policemen at the Fort, benefiting, he wrote, from the resentment they felt towards the secret police, or 'Special Branch', by whom they felt used. Thanks to this pencil, he was able to devise mathematical puzzles for himself on paper from slabs of chocolate sent into prison.

He was allowed to see my mother on family business, most of it 'occupied by her exhortations to stand firm'. Apart from this he was left in his cell during those 'long desert days', with nothing but his clothes and toiletries, no watch, no tie, no belt and, for reading matter, none of the newspapers he hungered for but only a Bible.

He was brought to trial in October 1964 and sentenced on 1 December of that year in terms of the Sabotage Act. Along with a small group of men and women making up the African Resistance Movement (ARM), he had been involved in Marxist discussion groups and the distribution of underground publications. This was followed, when all other means of resistance appeared to be impossible, by acts of sabotage: the blowing up of railway signal cables, power standards and, most dramatically, pylons, in the outlying areas of Johannesburg and Cape Town.

ARM members, often disaffiliated from various other groups, were by no means alone in believing that it was necessary to engage in such strategies. In the wake of the 1960 Sharpeville massacre, waves of revolt shook townships across the country. Political parties representing the disenfranchised majority were banned, and, as a result, activists of many persuasions turned to other, illegal ways of expressing their opposition. They argued that in this way they could encourage massive black unrest, while whites might finally begin to question what was happening all around them.

Pictures of ARM accomplishments appeared in the press: pylons resembling giant muscle-men lying helplessly mangled on their sides in bare stretches of veld, the accompanying reports incorrectly attributing their sorry state to sabotage by members of the African National Congress.

In the end, there was an ARM trial in Cape Town and another in Pretoria, where the accused were three white men, including my father. In an attempt to show, despite the evidence, that this was a whites-only movement, blacks were used as state witnesses whenever possible.

In court the mother of Raymond Eisenstein, one of the three, speaking through a Polish interpreter, described how she had smuggled her young son out of the Warsaw ghetto in a canvas bag while the Nazis burned their home.

Daantjie Oosthuizen, the philosophy professor who had taught the second man, Hugh Lewin, testified in his favour. He understood what Lewin had done, he said, because as a student he, too, had joined an underground organisation engaged in sabotage: the Ossewabrandwag, an extremist Afrikaner group bent on combating the British.

The main advocate for the defence, Arthur Chaskalson, took up this theme, tracing the history of dissent in South Africa, outlining the many cases of people, mainly Afrikaners, tried for subversion and sabotage, and stressing the leniency that had characterised their trials. He pleaded that the final judgment should not produce bitterness but rather give the convicted men a chance to hope.

In response, Judge Bekker stated: *The sentence which I am about to impose is one which I cannot reduce any further. To do so would, in my opinion, render the law a mockery.* Hugh Lewin and Raymond Eisenstein each received seven years – Eisenstein's sentence later being commuted – and my father two years more than that. At almost forty-three he was not only older but also senior to them in the ARM hierarchy. Eisenstein turned twenty-eight on the day he was sentenced, Lewin was about to turn twenty-five.

⁀

On the last day of the trial, after judgment had been passed, I was allowed to go with my mother to the courtroom in Pretoria. It was a deep, wide room, the air saturated with solemnity and heavy as stew, the lights not doing much against the dimness that hung between the wood-panelled walls.

Up in the public gallery, Granny Lily and her sister Essie sat with pale, talcum-powdered faces and pursed lips, black patent leather handbags held down fast against their laps. They greeted us and shook their heads, dismayed and grim and loving all at once.

At the far side of the room lawyers were gathering up their papers, tapping them neatly together against a tabletop. Others stood in a huddle, black robes swishing lightly against the floorboards.

I noticed the floorboards as I walked towards my father, they were polished so highly I could half see in them the deformed ceiling and the robes of the lawyers, like curtains I had to part.

Why was he standing there alone, with no one going up to him? Only my mother was present as I buried my face in the woven texture of his jacket and the olive-and-leather smell of his skin.

Then it was her turn. The two of them walked off together a short distance and stood in each other's arms before the law came slicing down between them.

I could see my father's halting steps as he was led away. He reached the end of the floorboards and then went through the dark mouth of the doorway, into the land of absence.

Pylons. So my father's arrest had had to do with pylons.

Sometimes, from the back of a car, I would see them lined up one behind the other, massive and skeletal, crossing the wasteland outside Johannesburg, bearing the cables that would bring light to the city. Unless those cables were there to chain the pylons together. The ones I passed were all still intact. I did not really allow myself to think about what my father might have done to them until one day in the classroom at high school.

We were reading a poem by Stanley Snaith written in 1933, when pylons had only just started making an appearance across England's gentle meadows.

[...] outposts of the trekking future.
Into the thatch-hung consciousness of hamlets
They blaze new thoughts, new habits.

I sat at my desk in school uniform among some thirty other boys, and as the teacher was reading the poem there came into my mind an image of my father. He was dressed in black leather (I had never seen him dressed in leather, nor anything black at all, for that matter; brown and grey, tan and a touch of olive green were more his style).

He was standing full-length in a speeding convertible car with some other people in the middle of the night (I had never seen him in a convertible car, either, let alone standing up in one. When he was at the wheel, he rarely travelled faster than about 50 miles an hour). Wind swept against their elated faces, their arms were raised to the stars (I had never seen my father join with anyone in making such an exuberant gesture), while behind them a pylon sank down slowly to its knees in a candescent blaze of flame.

Eventually, I learned more about what had really happened, who had done what, as well as details of the trial. These are recorded in books by my father and by Hugh Lewin. In one of his poems, Lewin gives a graphic description of fixing a packet of dynamite to a timing device at the base of a pylon out in the veld at night:

> [...]
> Big bastard, isn't he?
>
> And now, set? Set.
> If there's anything wrong here
> this'll blast us with it. Set
> and now, carefully, plug
>   in.
>
>   O.K.
>
> Above the throbbing and the hum
> you can feel the quiet ticking
> and grass seeds begin to itch.
>
> Let's go.
>
> Tomorrow morning, big boy, you'll blow.

In fact my father, older than most of the others he was associated with and handicapped by gout, had not participated in the actual blowing up of pylons at all, though as one of the leaders of the 'military committee' of the ARM he was involved in this activity at the planning stage.

It took many years for me to learn that, by the time of his arrest, his political ideas had changed: he had come to believe that sabotage was no longer an effective strategy, preferring to concentrate on ways of helping to organise black workers. But by then he had already done enough to be imprisoned as an enemy of the state.

⌒

Many years later, I sought out further information from two people who had been members of the ARM, both of them visitors to my boyhood home in Johannesburg.

The first was Raymond Eisenstein, a man by then in his 80s with a round, juvenile face, easy smile and boyish, mischievous voice, very clear about why he had done what he had done.

In those years we were at least a flicker of light and in some ways a lot more, he said. *If you compare the atmospheres and activities of the time to, say, France or Poland during the war, it was quite similar, really: there were groups not that different from the ARM waving a flag of hope.*

We were happy, perhaps even elated, after the Rand Daily Mail *published in a big splash a photo of the huge Bapsfontein pylon we had just brought down. And there were others, too.*

We hoped that our actions might in time deter investment decisions. And the ARM also saved lives. The apartheid regime used to banish Africans, especially those from the rural areas who opposed it. These were eminent people, often tribal chiefs, who were deported to remote and totally isolated areas outside of their tribal lands. We rescued many of them, taking them on dangerous roads outside of the country to a more liveable situation. That alone, in my view, would justify what we did.

I played a typical woman's role, Bernice Laschinger told me on the phone. Barely twenty years old at the time and a student at the University of the Witwatersrand in Johannesburg, she had gone to my father's office in the physics department there, packed together explosives and smuggled them out in biscuit tins.

She knew full well why she was a member of this group of people: *We all felt the need to act urgently. It was such a bleak, oppressive time after Sharpeville. We had to show that resistance was still alive. And create a hostile environment so investors would think twice about South Africa.*

Nor did her role end with biscuit tins, because at night she went driving out of Johannesburg, then sat in Raymond Eisenstein's arms at the back of a car in the dark, on edge with adrenalin and terror in case a police car came by. They were there to divert attention from two other people, Flip Green and Denis Higgs, both out in the veld just a brief sprint away, that very moment busy planting dynamite at the base of a pylon.

One night in January 1965, a few months after my father's trial, there was a knock at our front door. My mother wasn't expecting anyone, not that late; it turned out to be a man we knew.

He did not have much time, apparently, but he nonetheless settled against the little maroon roses of our settee, sipping at a cup of tea as he told us my father was fighting fit, he knew because he himself had just been released from a neighbouring cell in the same prison.

Everything about him irritated me, from the clearly relieved expression on his face to the bad cut of his trousers and the way he sat there munching Romany Creams. I wanted him out of there like the couple of copper-coloured rose-beetles he had let into the room and that went endlessly, crazily knocking against all the lights.

I could almost smell darkness on him, the same darkness that loomed up around me every time I thought of my father. Then again, if this man was able to emerge from his cell to be there with us, then why not my father himself? What was this man doing in his place? When was he going to stop speaking and smiling and bringing my father's absence so impossibly close?

He turned out to be only a precursor. All in all, twenty-three white male political prisoners filled the maximum security section of Pretoria Local Prison in the mid-1960s, and several of them – whom my mother and I had never previously met – made a point of seeing us upon their release, delivering messages from my father.

One sat with us on the grass of a park, holding onto himself as if the turning world made him dizzy, glancing unsteadily around, every bush bristling with someone who wasn't there but could leap out and arrest him all over again.

One stood amongst the jumbled furniture of a room, in the quake of leaving the country, and spoke too quietly, his voice the echo of an echo of what it might once have been as he repeated, like all the others, that everyone in prison was all right, and repeated it just one too many times.

Another, handsome and younger than the rest, went swimming smooth as a seal in his lawyer's pool, cleansing himself length after length, lying out on the warm tiles at the ruffled water-side, leaving his shadow printed there as he stood up against the vast blue sky.

Occasionally we met more of them, but for only a few moments because they were always running out of time; there was a plane just about to take off in the direction of exile. Each one had the same message: everything was fine inside, just hunky-dory. Patience was all we needed, not too long for us to wait now.

But they themselves were famished. Absence still lay thick upon their ill-fitting clothes and clipped hair, lined brows and concave cheeks, and above all in their gaze that had not yet returned to the outside world.

They threaded a kind of intermittent procession through our lives, this straggling, motley crew of men, of varied political affiliation, yet all of them officially portrayed as renegades and outcasts and traitors to the white South African world. Despite the ideological discord that divided them from each other, they had been bonded into a sort of community, pitted against the prison authorities in particular and the regime in general.

They considered my mother and me to be of their kind, long before I had any clear political ideas of my own.

Politics for me, at the time, meant nothing but personal loss; I am not sure that it meant much more to my mother.

As for community, I had no sense of belonging to

one, either political or of any other sort. Yet despite myself, as of those early weeks of my father's arrest and that first visit to him, I was blooded into the margins of the place I lived in, brought into premature wakefulness by my shaky knowledge of what those ex-prisoners had done, and why.

After the end of his trial, at the beginning of December 1964, the next time I saw my father was three years later, when I turned sixteen – the age at which it was legally possible to enter a prison.

I visited him in the company of my mother, at progressively shorter intervals: every six weeks, then after some time every month, and towards the end of his sentence every fortnight. My brother and sister, on the other hand, saw him only once during the nine and a half years of his imprisonment.

The visits were like going to another country. Get dressed, comb your hair, collect your thoughts, but quickly. Watch the clock. Then drive out under the trees of Johannesburg, past Benny Goldberg's bottle store to the left, and to the right the shacks of Alexandra Township with rocks holding down their corrugated-iron roofs; then dry scrub, the occasional cow, Halfway House, and finally, on the outskirts of Pretoria, that place past the far edge of our daily lives, out of sight, off the map: the land of absence, where everything was otherness and yet clocks were set to the same time as ours.

It took sixty-five kilometres to get to Pretoria Local Prison, no highway, lots of trucks, how was it possible that there were always so many of them out on the road on a Saturday afternoon? My mother, only recently in possession of her driver's licence, had yet to master the art of overtaking. So we left home about two hours in advance of the visit itself and were regularly escorted there by a selection of the rustiest and least roadworthy vehicles in the country.

We sat in the car in vacuum-packed silence, windows closed to keep out the din and exhaust fumes, my mother holding onto the steering wheel for dear life while going over what she was about to say to her husband. Too often, in the thick of the tension a dogfight broke out between us, after which I would placate her with crescent-moons of naartjie or shreds of dried mango and peach.

High above the scab-red brick of the prison buildings, in the watchtower, a dim spectacle of guards armed with rifles and Alsatians. In the waiting room, a burnt offering of cigarette stubs, in a wide aluminium ashtray, adding their stench to the corrosive reek of Jeyes Fluid and the sweat of despair.

A prelude of clanging gates and then my father emerged with his guard from the far end of the next-door visiting room, in faded khaki topped with a neat brown corduroy jacket. He came towards us limping because of the gout, in his slimmed-down body because of the meagre food and obligatory exercise, with his brave hangdog smile because what other expression could he wear upon his face on such an occasion.

For thirty serrated minutes and not a second longer he stood before us at a narrow panel of plexiglass, with a piece of wood sticking up from its waist-height base at 60° to prevent us from showing him any notes concerning the world news he hungered for but was not allowed to receive.

Our halting conversation took place with a guard breathing at our shoulders on either side. It was strung together with sentences either stretched out too long or knotted and shrunk far too short, the frustration on my father's face following us home as if imprinted in the rear-view mirror of our car.

Did children of other political prisoners live through this period of their lives in the same way that I did?

I met some of them, but we did not speak of such things.

We smiled at each other, the zipped-up smile of defensiveness and pride I think we had all learned, with

Denis Hirson

a hint of complicity mixed in: we all knew we were living in the company of the shadow of that Other Place. It woke up with us, ate with us at table, filtered the sunlight during holidays, sat at the fireside in the Highveld winter, went pacing through our dreams.

Two of those children stayed at our home for a while. Their names were Jill and Peter Schermbrucker. Their father, Ivan, had been arrested for underground activities against apartheid. So had their mother, Leslie. And from her prison in Barberton, 190 miles to the east of Johannesburg, Leslie once sent us a gift of a khaki drill-cotton book-cover, embroidered by herself.

On the front of this cover was the head of a lady with smiling eyes and a mouth set in an expression of lean determination. Her narrow face was embroidered in black thread; unkempt strands of her violet hair came rippling outwards like a wild crown, the whole image constrained within a black, violet and sienna-red frame. Onto the inside fold of the cover were sewn in black the words 'WITH BEST WISHES', and below them, in dark brown: BARBERTON '67.

I had just finished my last year of high school, and found that the cover almost perfectly fitted the Bible I had been required to buy for the religious instruction class there.

For most of that class, my classmates and I had been instructed to colour in passages from both the New and Old Testaments, using a red crayon.

Our teacher, who was rumoured to have once killed another man in the course of a boxing match, would start off by urging us, his voice dripping with sentiment, to follow a virtuous path.

He then named the page we were to turn to, chapter and verse, read out a few lines, and spent the rest of the period checking that we were making assiduous use of our crayons. But it was the quietest class of the day, and there was time to take in the passages as they went under their fresh red colour.

Oh my God, I cry in the daytime, but thou hearest not; and in the night season, and am not silent.

When I consider thy heavens, the work of thy fingers, the moon and the stars, which thou hast ordained; what is man, that thou art mindful of him? And the son of man, that thou visitest him?

Neither do men light a candle, and put it under a bushel, but on a candlestick; and it giveth light unto all that are in the house.

For now we see through a glass, darkly; but then face to face: now I know in part; but then shall I know even as also I am known.

With their solemn yet elusive beauty and their breadth, their exhortations and threats and the ancient solemnity of their song, the words turned red as my hand worked at the page, from there entering the chamber of myself, resonating in the name of a belief I did not have.

As for the Bible itself, I wrapped it in that cloth cover stitched as an act of resistance, the woman on the front still shaking her violet hair free of the confines of prison.

More than forty years later, in 2010, when my son Jeremy had his bar mitzvah, I presented this same Bible to him, its pages still patched with red crayon marks, its cloth cover stitched with the filaments of embroidery from out of that embattled time.

Part Two

The Egg Scale

One

Of course I did not tell myself, in the aftermath of my special thirteenth birthday visit, that I had had a bar mitzvah. I was never going to have a bar mitzvah in the first place, so I had not prepared for one in any way.

Besides, who has a bar mitzvah in a car with two policemen in the front seats? What an unholy mess of a situation, with my father sitting next to me but not even able to say, let alone do, what he wanted, plucked out of his daze of solitary confinement, suspended helplessly for thirty minutes beyond the walls of his cell.

There he was, displayed in all his misery before his eldest son, his wife beyond reach and out of earshot yet only a dozen paces away. And his two other children, far too young at that stage to understand what was going on, miles off in the distant everyday world that was turning without him.

That, at least, was one way of seeing how things had been. But I did not describe them to myself in those terms at the time. I failed to describe them in any terms at all, whether to myself or anyone else.

Instead, I packed the memory of the event in the ice of my mind and froze it before words could get there, because naming everything would have meant seeing the details all over again, dangling them before my own eyes until I could take on their composite meaning and disastrous consequence, and this I was entirely incapable of doing.

Nor was there anyone to remind me afterwards of what had happened in that car, or relate it to me from a different perspective. In the wake of a big birthday celebration one might expect others who had been there to say how *they* had experienced it all, the key moments, the guests, the music, a racy joke overheard during the meal. There could have been flashbulb photos or at least phone calls, some other trace.

But no one spoke to me of the visit to my father. I did not know how to share such things with my mother. And besides, as she sat in that other car on the tarmac, she must have had emotions of her own. It was the last thing I wanted to speak about to my friends. And as for my father, he was prohibited from writing letters in the period preceding his trial, nor did I see him for the following three years.

So I emerged from that afternoon alone, with my own impressions and no one else's. The next day there was school again, and the day after that the same, which was fortunate because it was much easier to think of Bunsen burners or logarithms or a crocodile lying at the bottom of a pool in an Afrikaans poem, than of what had recently happened for thirty minutes in a cramped-up car in a prison parking lot.

If, at the time, anyone had suggested that that visit might ultimately do me some good, or mark my passage into manhood, or that many years later I would want to sift through my memories in case they yielded a ray or two of light, then I would simply have looked at them in blank disbelief.

⌒

Let me repeat, though, as before: of course I had a bar mitzvah.

Nothing that has ever happened need always be seen in exactly the same way.

Time passes, and for some reason, at an unforeseen moment, the spirit bends in an unexpected direction. New people appear on the horizon, the horizon itself changes shape. With any luck, perhaps even with the lever of love, some stone blocking the view is removed from one's inner landscape and the past appears in a different light.

In the case of this story the key person concerned was my daughter. But many years before I ever imagined having a daughter, or even dreamed of meeting someone I might have a daughter with, one Saturday evening in June 1970 while I was still living in Johannesburg, something happened that was going to be of great importance to me.

Call it fate, or the finest of accidents, or perhaps the winds of chance were blowing as I drove out northwards to a suburb of the city I had never visited before, then parked outside a house belonging to the parents of a girl I had barely ever spoken to.

It is true that I had noticed her sitting out on the library lawn of our university campus. She had long, glossy dark hair and a beautiful oval face hidden behind a pair of wide-framed glasses. She seemed to be generally pensive and shy, but she was very different on that particular evening.

She had decided to leave South Africa, this was her farewell party and it was in full swing. On entering the basement I found tens of guests already bobbing up and down to the music of the Beatles.

There she was among them, her face wide open, eyes sparkling, cheeks flushed. At one point Paul McCartney began singing 'Penny Lane', the piccolo trumpet burst forth from the playful nostalgia of the song, and by then I was dancing with her.

Had she not been glowing with the distinctly loose-ended energy of one who is about to take off and find her own way in the world, then I might not have approached her, while she for her part might never have allowed our lips to touch.

But they did, and the kiss remained as a bond

between us. After that party we met again. On one occasion, when my mother was unable to go on our thirty-minute monthly visit to my father in Pretoria Local Prison, that girl came with me.

Later, we sent each other letters describing our new lives: a few years after she had left South Africa, I did too. My father was released at the end of November 1973. Our whole family sailed with him to England and settled in London.

Then one day I phoned her from there.

She was living in Paris with her boyfriend.

Can I come and see you? I asked.

Yes, she answered with not a moment's hesitation.

It was one of the sweetest words I had heard in a while. I was still wrapped up in the parcel of what had happened during those prison years. And I was still living with the first woman I had ever loved, who had come over to join me in England from out of my old life in South Africa, though I eventually realised I was not ripe enough to be with anyone at all; still confused about what to do with myself, or where to turn, or why.

But now, one night at the end of March 1975, I set my red backpack down on the deck of the ferry crossing the Channel, then caught the train from Calais to Paris. It was only a matter of hours before I was going underground to step into the dull pond-green métro with its rattling wheels and slatted wooden seats, some of them still reserved for war invalids.

It was quite early in the morning and I noticed only one other person in the carriage: a man sitting near me wearing shiny glasses, a worn leather briefcase at his side. He must have been on the way to work though he had on a short-sleeved shirt and no jacket, and the bronzed skin of his arms seemed to be breathing.

I, too, was breathing. Lost and lovesick, but breathing.

Pasted to a wall of the métro station where I got out, a poster announced in big red letters that for the sake of one's health one should not drink more than a litre of wine a day. At street level, spring light came spilling across the pale façades before me, so fresh a cat could have stalked up and licked it.

My friend and her companion came to the door in their dressing gowns to give me a foggy welcome: it was not yet 7am. But I was entirely awake. I could have climbed any number of freshly waxed stairs to see from their window the terracotta chimney pots like binoculars looking up at the sky.

Even the soap in the shower had the perfume of another world.

After a few weeks, I still had little idea of how long I was going to stay. And if I left, where was it that I could think of going? The needle of my inner compass was not pointing anywhere, my one star was indecision, my only wish to distance myself from where I had been.

One afternoon, I was sitting on a Paris bus opposite a boy of five or six years old. He was reciting by heart, to a benevolent-looking woman who might have been his grandmother, something which I could not immediately decipher. I eventually realised that it was the alphabet, though, despite the familiar rhythm and some of the rhymes, most of it sounded all wrong.

It simply had not occurred to me that the names of the letters of the alphabet might make different sounds in French from their equivalents in English. But then I myself was no more than a five- or six-year-old adult, learning the ropes of another world, crossing the frontier into a new language.

I no longer wanted to speak English. One morning out in the street, on hearing a couple of English-speaking tourists desperately asking their way, I refused, like some obtuse Parisian, to reveal that I knew both what they meant and how to get to where they wanted to go.

The locals, however, could immediately tell that I was not one of them. When, after many months, I at last opened my mouth in an attempt to speak in more or less full sentences, out came broken, bad, rudimentary French, some of which I remembered from high school. But it was riddled with errors of gender, lacking in the subjunctive, yawning with open vowel sounds when they should have been neatly pursed, the 'r' grinding in my throat when a native-speaker rolled it out with the agility of a moped.

The French language is considered to be a national treasure, its sonority finely chiselled and its sense shining with clarity. On hearing me, people would wince as they might have on discovering a worm in a roast chestnut they had just bitten into.

Vous avez un petit accent, they would say, literally 'you have a little accent', meaning that my foreignness was blaring at them as if through a megaphone, this remark being followed by the inevitable question as to where I came from.

Sometimes the conversation, in French, went something like this:

Where do you come from?
South Africa.
Oh, they would say.
Pause.
But which country in South Africa?
South Africa is the name of a country. At the southern tip of Africa.
Ah, they would say.

Pause.

Then: *What kind of food do people eat there?*

I did, however, meet many people in Paris who knew perfectly well about the current political situation in South Africa. It was the mid-1970s. There were meetings, speeches, protests outside the tank-like South African Embassy, but nothing on the scale of the massive demonstrations at Trafalgar Square or the campaign against South African products such as Outspan oranges in England, drummed up by the exile community there.

England might have been six thousand miles from South Africa, but France felt as if it were much, much further away.

So much the better.

I needed to be as far away as possible.

☙

The unknown city was spread out all around me. I would wake up and go out into the streets, hardly aware of where I was on the map, not opening any guidebook, as if wanting knowledge of Paris to enter my bloodstream through the soles of my shoes.

Such a dense and intricate city, turning on the axis of a majestic river whose waters were constantly changing colour, from glittery steel to chunks of jade and murky, chocolate mud. Such a complex gathering of quarters: to the west, elegant passers-by, lean as baguettes, to whom geraniums blew kisses from high balconies; to the east, on a Sunday morning, away from the modest white locals, men in the dull garb of the 1950s sitting close together in immigrant complicity, on benches that could have come with them from a North African village.

In the centre such early morning high-strung bustle, followed by long lunchtimes in bistros that spilled out onto pavement terraces; people buying books and records, silk scarves and perfume in their free time, smoking as they strolled through rigidly geometrical parks where a guard would blow a whistle if you stepped on the grass. And everywhere traffic manoeuvring with a din like dodgems, down avenues and narrow streets and across roundabouts shaped like stars.

A proud city, fuelled on potent black coffee for the day ahead yet glancing backwards into the evening of a past that was present everywhere: in ancient walls and slender arches, old stone bridges, massive carriage doors opening to reveal the secretive, luminous tranquillity of courtyards from another age.

History was concealed in the names of streets and buildings and metro stations, in statues, plaques, monuments, gravestones, cobblestones. There were granite paving stones in the middle of the road where a guillotine had stood, a Roman arena and Roman baths, inscriptions in flagstones, shrapnel-holes in walls through which the past spoke.

In the quarter of the Marais, archaic signs were displayed for shop-front synagogues, next door to stationery shops whose windows were cluttered with Holy Land paraphernalia and bakeries filled with the Eastern European memory of moist cheesecake and apple strudel; dark, sour bread rich with rye.

Jews drifted along in clothes sewn out of the heavy shadows of ancestry, light turning sepia upon the narrow streets they towed behind them.

I did not see how they could have anything to do with me.

Two

During those first months in Paris, I repeatedly saw in my mind's eye a man in a boat with a small tree growing in front of him.

Rowing, rowing, no land in sight.

No waves, barely any movement of the oars.

No sail.

No wind.

No water.

Yet the man went on sitting in that boat as if its compact, elongated shape were an extension of his body.

Barely stirring.

Going nowhere.

Unable to see where the tree was planted, though it faced him on the deck, its leaves all green.

He went on rowing, with his tree for company.

⌒

In the summer of 1976, more than a year after my arrival in Paris, I decided to go to Israel for a few weeks. Why not travel around the country and get to know my mother's family again, meet up with my grandparents, my uncles and aunts and cousins? After all, I had not seen them for more than thirteen years.

So I did that, finally arriving, suitably tanned and wearing my new indestructible Israeli sandals, at my grandparents' home for the last few days. They were now living in Jerusalem, in an old block of flats with walls of pale stone, on a shady street lined with fragrant pine trees.

Quite early in the morning I would catch the bus and go out, particularly into the Old City. But by lunchtime I was usually back, taking refuge from the heat of the day in Toba's small, cool kitchen as she prepared breaded aubergine or mince-balls or barley soup for a meal. All the while, she would be singing a Russian or Yiddish song with a dash of wild relish and scant respect for the tune.

Her face looked like no one else's in our family. There was pride in it, a degree of distance from those around her, and a streak of repressed drama in the set of her mouth. Her manner was almost curt; she was preoccupied with her health, and cooking, and my grandfather Zalman.

One afternoon, though, as we sat at the lunch table, she started telling me stories about her past. *Los op, Toba* (Just stop that), Zalman mumbled at her in Yiddish, but she wouldn't. *Bubbe-meises* (grandmother's fables), he grumbled, but she brushed him aside.

At first what she was saying remained remote and exotic to me, but if she noticed this then she nevertheless persisted. We would have a meal, ending with some hot but bland and virtually tasteless Wissotzky tea; Zalman left the room and Toba would pick up where she had left off. If Zalman wandered back to the kitchen, interrupting her again, then she paid him no attention. She knew a famished listener when she found one.

Before the next summer holidays I bought a solid tape-recorder and a microphone along with a metal suitcase in which to lug them back to Jerusalem. In the afternoon I set everything up on the oilcloth of the kitchen table. Toba would sit down next to me and start speaking, until she started turning from a woman in her seventies into a little girl, living in a big wooden house in a shtetl outside Minsk in the early years of the twentieth century.

There were slabs of ice cut from the river to keep food fresh in the kitchen; a fire set under the metal bath to heat the water. In the shed, barrel upon barrel of salted cowhides – a currency more stable than money – earned by her father the schochet for his services.

There she was, crouched behind an armchair so her father would not see her, scrutinising every detail as he inflated the lungs of a cow to make sure the meat was healthy.

Some years later there she was again, the oldest child, wearing her best dress as she had been told to, sitting with her parents and six siblings at their long dinner table. Also present were two specially invited guests, a father and son, who had arrived that evening in a 'hossnkat' (there were lots of 'hossnkats' in Toba's stories, they turned out to be horse-drawn carts; in fact the whole English language was crunched and oiled and flipped in her Yiddish frying pan).

Noticing how the guests were both deliberately looking her up and down, she ducked under the table and escaped from the room. She knew where she stood when it came to arranged marriages. *Already I was ahead*, she said.

Soon it was 1917 and the air was filled with Bolshevik ideas. Children began leaving home, some even betraying their parents to the authorities. Whereas her father's word had been law, now this square-shouldered, blond-haired, blue-eyed man, pillar of her life, was beginning to be frightened. Soon, still defending his religion, his craft and his ritual knives, he would be exiled to Siberia. But by then, as a young woman, Toba had already made her way to Odessa, and from there by boat to Palestine, where she eventually met Zalman.

Vit his eyes he took me, she said. *Vot forra hendsum men he voz.*

I grew a little jealous of this 'hendsum men' who

now, competing with his wife, brought a diary no one had heard of before from the back of a wardrobe. So now I learned how he had survived the First World War as a Russian foot soldier, ducking bullets, eating shrivelled potatoes in the snow; returned to a shtetl outside Minsk (not Toba's) and from there escaped to Palestine where he eventually met up with her.

Above their Jerusalem bed was hung a wedding photograph that showed them, eyes liquid with dreaming, heads tilted together as if magnetised. How fortunate he had been, I thought, to spend a lifetime in the company of this woman whom I found beautiful though her skin was no longer creamy-clear, the chestnut thickness of her hair changed to silver filament.

If I was entranced, I was also faced with her scatty and unpredictable nature. Her stories were tangled with contradictions and it took days to try and unknot them. But never mind. Even if I ended up with three or four conflicting versions of the same set of events, they were all nonetheless part of how my mother's mother's life had been. I was twenty-six years old and I was beginning to not only understand, but to feel from under my skin, that I and my family actually had a past.

I soaked in this knowledge from the lips of my grandmother, accompanied by the music of her voice and the fullness of her forest-brown gaze.

I cannot say how close we came to each other over the five or six visits I paid her as an adult, but my need to listen to her was at least equal to her need to tell me how she had come to be the person she was. And telling her stories was like planting a tree in a field of love.

Where do you come from? people would ask me in Paris on hearing my accent.

South Africa, I replied.

I was born in England, but remember nothing of that, having arrived in South Africa before the age of two. There is no other country I can really say I come from. Nor will I ever be an ex-South African, any more than I will be an ex-child, ex-son, ex-father, ex-immigrant. I am all the things I have become. South Africa swarms in my memories, my family, my friendships, my reading, my writing; my ineradicable accent, which I have no wish to eradicate.

Unless it is Johannesburg I come from, place of my first remembered home and uprooting; first love, first words, first wounds. What, after all, does it mean to come from a country that was – at the time when I was growing up there – broken up into so many ill-fitting, walled-off fragments of territory, unequal in all ways, with most people denied full citizenship, and yet with a single illusory flag and anthem?

How, as young adults, we all held onto that city, or was it the whole country?

How could we simply pack our bags and leave 'the situation' as it was behind us?

What were we supposed to with the still wet umbilical cord of our white guilt?

And then there were those lines from CP Cavafy's poem 'The City' that followed me around like a curse:

[...] You will not find new lands, not find another sea.
The city will follow you. You'll wander down these very streets, age in these same quarters of the town,
among the same houses finally turn grey.
You'll reach this city always. Don't hope to get away [...]

But beyond our need to deal with unfinished business, many of us did get away. And it was from afar that the question of where we came from began to sound differently. Strangers in a strange land do not wear their identities in the same way as those who have never settled outside the place of their childhood.

Where *did* we come from in the end, once we had discovered that our lives were intimately linked to those of people who had come from so many other places, nervously skipping their way to the perilous music of history?

Toba and Zalman had run a life-threatening gauntlet to escape the pogroms of what was then Russia to reach Palestine, then spent twenty years in South Africa – *sitting on our suitcases*, said Toba – before returning to Israel as soon as it was declared a state.

My mother, born to them in Palestine and arriving in South Africa by ship at the age of two, would never have said that she came from South Africa.

My father's mother arrived in South Africa from a shtetl outside Riga, in Latvia, at the age of three. Her husband Joe had come from nearby. I doubt that either of them, from out of the limbo of their Johannesburg lives, would have said that they came from South Africa.

It was my father, born in Johannesburg, who planted himself there through his underground political engagement, living by his set of beliefs and his moral compass, more than a drop of bloody-minded obsession and a pinch of despair. By the meaning and consequence of his actions, and by the wound of his absence, he rooted his eldest son.

I come from South Africa, but once I had left the country, what I needed to know – and the knowledge altered the way I told my own story – was that our family line stretched backwards into a past of other places. And if it did so then it could stretch forwards as well, through England and France to who knew where.

⤸

During one of my visits to Israel, I had asked to see more closely an object in Toba's kitchen. It was high up on a shelf, above the pots and pans and Ball jars of stewed quinces glowing in their amber syrup.

It looked like a fantailed bird with a pertly raised but featureless head, about the size of an outstretched adult hand, made of iron and standing on three legs. The head was in fact a cup in which to place an egg, because the object was an egg scale; the tail was a curved, graduated, sliding scale which gave the egg's weight, looking a bit like a sailor's sextant.

But if it really was useful, then what was it doing perched on high, collecting dust? Had I given that egg scale a second thought, its position up there might have told me something about the shaky relationship between my grandmother and poultry.

Toba, on being asked, made no bones about the fact that her attempts to raise poultry, however ambitious, first in South Africa and then Israel, had been catastrophic from the start. The epic started off in the 1930s in a backyard in Johannesburg, with her using ammonia to clean a hutch full of chickens because she thought they were dirty. Their heads started drooping so she fed them castor oil, but they died all the same. Then, after returning to what was now Israel, at a time of food rationing she obtained a whole crate full of chickens and they, too, soon gave up the ghost.

She did learn to inject them under a wing, drench them with eye-drops, light paraffin heaters to keep day-olds alive, watching over them all night so they would not burn themselves to death. Yet anyone could tell that, even if eggs became part of Toba and Zalman's livelihood for a short while, she was not in any way cut out for chickens, or turkeys, not in fact adapted to country life at all.

As for the egg scale, I rescued it from her kitchen shelf, attracted by its form and its function, not knowing that later I would see it as an heirloom, to be passed on at a key moment and woven into someone else's story.

Three

It was a Sunday morning in April 2004. Spring light filled the tall windows of our home just outside Paris. I was sitting at our kitchen table with my wife Adine, my daughter Anna, and a man named Oded Eldad. Outside, hopping among the charcoal-coloured, widespread branches of the Judas tree, a magpie shot at the quietness with the artillery of its voice.

My garden, said the magpie. *Ratatat tat. Get out. This garden is mine.*

Some say it is called the Judas tree because the seedpods dangle in a way that Judas Iscariot was supposed to have done after hanging himself from a tree of this kind. Others claim that the English name is derived from the French 'arbre de Judée', the tree of Judea, referring to the dry, hilly region around Jerusalem where this species grows.

In May its petals always make a cloud of colour outside the house, filled with suckling bees. Now the buds were beginning to open their narrow, delicate, dusty-mauve mouths.

But I wasn't opening mine.

Anna, aged eleven, had just told us which biblical text she intended to study for her bat mitzvah. She then went on to explain the reasons for her choice.

I sat there listening but could not speak: what she had to say was too close to the bone.

My wife Adine looked at me, my sweetly ferocious wife.

By the end of that meeting her eyes were smouldering upon me.

She knew I needed to break out of my silence, but I was not able to.

With the rattling machine-gun of its voice, the magpie continued to proclaim its territory out in the splash of spring sunlight.

Anna, the eldest of our two children and the first grandchild on both sides of the family, was drawn into a whirl of preparations for the ceremony she would be sharing with six other girls and four boys.

She studded the pages of an album with two genealogical trees and photographs of family members, six generations deep, on Adine's side and my own.

She produced a commentary on a biblical passage (Proverbs Ch.6 verses 16 to 19) in which the Lord is said to hate seven kinds of behaviour: pride, lying, 'hands that shed innocent blood, an heart that deviseth wicked imaginations', those who indulge in mischief or bear false witness 'and he that soweth discord among bretheren'. She ended her text with the following question: 'If there are so many things that God hates, and he does nothing about them, then I ask you: what kind of God is he?'

Like other grandparents of children in the group, Anna's two grandmothers (both her grandfathers by then no longer alive) were invited from England and the USA to tell stories of their own experience to the whole group of children and their parents. It was hoped that these stories might illuminate a human issue, perhaps a Jewish one, linking it to themes the children had been exploring together.

Adine's mother spoke, in impeccable French, of how she had escaped from Brussels and crossed France in a car with her family when the German bombs started falling in 1940. My mother, reading from a carefully prepared text, described how as a seven-year-old girl she had seen her mother crying on learning that her parents had been sent to Siberia, ending what she had to say like this:

> When I was a girl, although I was born in Palestine, and was growing up in South Africa, it seemed to me that I myself had lived in Russia; or rather, it seemed that I had grown up, not

in Russia, but out of Russia. My mother's past became my own past.

And this idea seemed to take root at a very particular time, when my grandfather was sent into exile.

We were invited to a series of get-togethers along with the rest of the group, where we discussed stories from Old Testament texts and participated in activities that brought different families face to face.

So there we were, Adine and I, immigrants though neither of us believed we fitted into any such category, but what were we then, long-term sojourners, settlers-by-chance, residents-by-desire, living our adopted French lives. And there was our daughter, engaged in a quest for ancestral bearings and deeper meaning at a time when she was taking her early steps towards womanhood.

On that Sunday morning when Anna announced to us which biblical text she would be working on, the fourth person sitting at our kitchen table, Oded Eldad, was the man who had conceived of the secular ceremony Anna would soon be going through.

In his seventies, with a charming and engaging presence, Oded was at the heart of the proceedings leading up to the event itself. Though his family was from Tunisia, he happened to have studied social anthropology in South Africa. He also had a deep interest in Jewish philosophy, and in the understanding of biblical stories as ways of revealing essentially human predicaments.

Anna, unusually hesitant at first but encouraged by Oded's laughing eyes and softly nudging voice, announced that she wanted to work on the passage where God asks Abraham to sacrifice his son Isaac.

That is what her grandfather had done, she went on to say: he had sacrificed his son for his ideals.

He should not have, she said.

Then she turned and looked at me.

She could not, she added, imagine that her own father would sacrifice his children in the same way.

⚛

I took out a Bible to read the story of Abraham and Isaac, Genesis Chapter 22:

> And it came to pass after these things, that God did tempt Abraham, and said unto him, Abraham: and he said, Behold, here I am. And he said, Take now thy son, thine only son Isaac, whom thou lovest, and get thee into the land of Moriah; and offer him there for a burnt

offering upon one of the mountains which I
will tell thee of.

The story takes less than a page, beginning with
Abraham embarking on the three-day journey
towards Moriah with his son, two other young men
and an ass. It ends with the angel of the Lord calling
unto the obedient Abraham out of heaven, and a
ram caught in a thicket by his horns replacing Isaac
as a sacrifice. The Lord is satisfied, and promises to
multiply Abraham's seed as the stars of heaven, and
as the sand which is upon the sea shore.

Before such a generous offer can be made, however,
Isaac has already lain down as he was told to, bound
upon the altar. Below his body, the woodpile that
Abraham had intended to set fire to after taking a
knife and slaying him.

There are few words, but they are pierced in every
syllable, as in the charged current of their syntax, with
an ancient, relentless light, trained upon a theatre of
faith and its near-disastrous consequences.

The curtain begins to close. We are told nothing
more of the boy, whether or not he is still motionlessly
bound up while the torch of fire goes on burning at
his side. Does he dwell upon what has just happened,
has his mind gone entirely numb, or do his thoughts
bear him as far away from his father and the altar as
possible?

Does he ask himself by what means that ram miraculously appeared out of nowhere?

Upon what slender thread of chance did his own life hang?

And can he not still see a knife in his father's empty hand?

Have his limbs not grown stiff, and are his nostrils not filled with the bitter smoke of the sacrificial fire?

Did he not witness his father slitting the ram's throat, and hear its cry, and breathe in the knowledge of his own death?

I knew the story already, but now, in case I had wanted to swerve away from looking at it more closely, my eleven-year-old daughter was sitting before me, demanding of me that I keep my eyes fixed upon that boy and his dire predicament.

꒰

Though Anna was not aware of this, the story of Abraham and Isaac had already entered my life a decade before her birth, in 1982.

I had been in Florence that summer, staying at the flat of Italian friends who were away on holiday, and spent a fortnight wandering about on my own. One day I wanted to visit the Baptistery, opposite the cathedral in the city centre, but it was closed. So I walked around the iron railings of the octagonal marble structure, and came to a halt before the most sumptuous of its three sets of double-doors, the ones Michelangelo is said to have found so beautiful he named them 'the gates of paradise'.

These particular double-doors, on the east side, show ten square panels, five down each door: fifteenth-century bas-reliefs sculpted in bronze by Lorenzo Ghiberti, depicting various scenes from the Old Testament. In one panel, Abraham stands draped in his robes, knife raised against Isaac who kneels on the altar, head bent away from his father, arms behind his back. The angel has arrived in a swirl of cloud above them, stretching one hand out to stay the haft of the knife; the other points past Abraham's beard to the ram sitting demurely on a nearby ledge, which will soon be sacrificed in Isaac's stead.

Not long after my visit to the Baptistery I had a dream: I was standing at these doors, which were locked against me. But in the dream, Isaac was not yet bound up and Abraham was still leading him uphill towards the altar, both of them alive in molten bronze.

I had to pass through the doors. So I raised a sword in both hands, lunged downwards and split them apart. Behind them there stretched an endless night sky where a moon was suspended, full-cheeked and luminous, looking at me from out of my father's face.

Those were the unmistakable wings of his moustache below his prominent nose and square chin. That was his high forehead and sustained gaze. His head had been severed from his body, but he was radiant as he looked at me.

A *Jewish moon*, I woke up saying.

At that point, in 1982, my father had already been in London for more than eight years. Physically, that is. In spirit he continued to be drawn by a potent backwash of conviction into what was happening in South Africa. The white regime was pursuing its vicious policies there, in what was to be its final decade. The result was a torrent of bullets and bombs, states of emergency, arrests and banning orders, rigged prison suicides and political trials, kidnappings, hangings and assassinations.

Sometimes my father would be out earnestly lecturing on politics and history; sometimes he would enter the thick of debate in seminars and meetings, highly knowledgeable, sharp of mind and tongue, subject to sudden emotional overheating, blunt in his judgment of what was Right and Wrong. Always fighting for the Cause, yet recalcitrantly outside the bounds of any political party: 'a one-man struggle', a colleague of his once dubbed him.

After training himself in prison to become a historian, he was now also channelling his considerable energies into writing studies of twentieth-century resistance to the South African state, which would ultimately run all the way from the development of black trade unions in the 1930s to the Soweto revolt of 1976, and include an account of his own political engagement.

I would arrive from Paris to find him drawn into the world of his desk, which was thick with tomes and papers, letters, pamphlets, journals and files. A weighty computer hummed before him day and night; a few feet away, plants in plastic pots lined the windowsill, reaching for the London sky that glimmered through the curtains like light from a distant star.

We would exchange words for a short time about this or that, after which he would slip away into an enthusiastic description of the historical information he had recently dug up, including a slew of names and acronyms, events, places and dates.

He would move his hands around while speaking as if making space for them all so that they could burst into the present: for my father, history was alive, it was not only what had happened, but also what should have happened (if only he had been listened to at the time), and could still be conjured into happening (if he would only be listened to in the present).

My smile hurt my cheeks as I stood there listening

to him. Even worse than my cheeks were my shoulders. They tightened until they felt like lumps of lead on both sides of my neck, filling the dip of my clavicles.

This had been my physical reaction to him for years.

But was I not the loving son, and had my father's absence not made my heart grow considerably, endurably fonder? It would surely have been far easier that way. But as I came into his presence an undeniable weight descended upon me, as if from the sky. My boyhood sky, where my father had stood so tall for me, and then acted in such a way as to get himself arrested, leaving the air compressed and moulded against me.

In short, I was angry with him.

Inflamed with a muscular heat that was trapped in my shoulders and refused to be released.

Angry, with an old and stagnant anger, that he should have acted in such a way as to absent himself from me, from his whole family; silently raging at him, unable to unleash in his presence the words for my own emotion.

⁓

One night, I was in my parents' kitchen when my father came in to make himself a mug of instant coffee before returning to his computer.

The kettle started rumbling.

I wanted to speak to him and have him speak to me about the prison years. But I had not prepared myself for any such conversation, no doubt afraid of what I might unleash between us.

I opened my mouth, and the only words that came out were *I forgive you.*

He was stirring the instant coffee into boiled water, and looked up at me.

I cannot say what he thought at that moment.

I cannot even say whether he realised what it was I might want to forgive him for.

I could have taken the initiative and opened a dialogue between us, instead of starting at the end of a conversation the beginning of which we had not had, closing it off before it had begun. How could I speak of forgiveness before we had taken the time to speak through at least something of the way we had each lived through his prison years?

Was that a blank look on his face, because his thoughts were entirely elsewhere? Did he believe he had done anything for which he needed to be forgiven?

I cannot remember anything else that was said between us that night.

Like all other questions concerning our unshared past, this one was left buried under hard ground that neither of us was able to break, nor so much as begin to walk across.

How, under such circumstances, could I begin to speak to my father about Abraham and Isaac, a dream in Florence and a Jewish moon in a place of baptism?

Where was I supposed to begin? Like this, perhaps, if ever I had dared to:

Look, Dad, I was staying in Florence and I had this dream in which I saw an image of Abraham about to sacrifice Isaac, and I split the image apart with a sword.

The thing is, you did sacrifice me, didn't you? Without meaning to, no doubt, since your head was facing the direction of the Struggle.

But in the dream I was facing you. Armed, taking my manhood in hand.

Let's say this was my revenge.

Or that I broke through a spell concerning what had happened between us.

And you were decapitated.

Not that you were altogether unhappy about it, because in the end you were beaming at me.

The light at last returned between us.

In my dream.

You were the womanly moon, it bore your face and no one else's, looking down at me from out of the night sky, yellow and bright.

A Jewish moon, in fact.

That's what I said to myself when I woke up.
No, I can't explain why the moon should be Jewish.
But you are. And it was.
A Jewish moon up in the night sky.
Our sky.
Shining.
Free of the debt between us.
We could be.
With any luck.
Both of us.
Free of the years of sacrifice.

The idea of sacrifice was not uncommon in South Africa at the time of apartheid. I knew many people who had given years of their lives to the struggle against the state, and not only those who had served time in prison.

I knew two of them who been shot dead, one by a hit squad in the street outside his house, while the other had been standing at the window near where his thirteen-year-old daughter was sleeping, and died in her arms. I knew a woman who had opened a letter-bomb in her own kitchen and been blown apart, along with her six-year-old daughter.

Some of my closest friends had been arrested, at least one of them badly tortured. I had seen families suspended in limbo, torn with divorce or sunk in depression as they waited or would not, could not wait for a political prisoner to be released.

When was there ever a war without sacrifice? An almost sacred aura surrounded those who had given of their lives in the name of what they believed was right.

My daughter was not unaware of politics, even at the age of eleven, but was speaking of something else. She was concerned above all with love and the betrayal of love.

'Betrayal' had had another meaning in South Africa, riddled as it was in the years of apartheid with spies and defectors and those who sang, some of them even before they could be threatened with torture. My daughter, however, was drawing me back not to what my father had done out in the world, but to what had happened between him and myself in the intimacy of our relationship.

I had not mentioned my dream to her.

She had not known my father well, he died in London in 1999 when she was seven years old, and was most often absorbed in his work at his desk when we went over from Paris to see my parents. But she was aware of the prison years, had heard more than once the story of that meeting in the Volkswagen on my thirteenth birthday.

She was naming herself as a witness to events such as that one which she had not seen and yet had taken on inside herself; events that had occurred in what felt to me like another life, to someone I could not deny was myself, in places I had no wish to go back to, or not then anyway, certainly not that Sunday morning outside Paris at our kitchen table, with sunlight streaming in through the window and a magpie out in the Judas tree, raking our garden with the rapid fire of its voice.

I knew what had happened between myself and my father. Yet this knowledge had sunk immobile as a stone inside me, its full consequence for myself kept closed as a secret, which Anna had found out.

But this was *her* bat mitzvah, wasn't it?

How had she managed to rope me in, too?

⌒

On the afternoon of 5 July 2004, more than a hundred and twenty people packed into the hall of the Cercle Bernard Lazare, in the Parisian quarter of the Marais. Amongst them were Anna's two grandmothers and other family members from England, Israel and the United States. Lack of space limited the number of guests we could invite, but we were nonetheless able to include a few people who were part of the French family we had made for ourselves.

The lights had been dimmed; the atmosphere was crisp as cellophane paper with expectation.

The eleven children entered the hall, each carrying a candle, so that a line of small, wavering points of light went with them onto the stage. One by one they thanked their teacher, Oded, going on to speak of their parents and siblings, sometimes not uncritically, sometimes drawing laughter from the audience.

Then each child delivered a full commentary of the biblical passage he or she had studied.

When Anna's turn came, after addressing Adine and me, she told the story of Abraham and Isaac as she saw it, from the inside, following their actions and possible thoughts, beginning with the moment when Abraham is told that he must sacrifice his son, and ending like this:

Abraham puts Isaac, his son, on the altar, upon the wood, and binds him.

Abraham stretches out his hand because he wants to get everything over with so that his child will suffer as little as possible [...].

God promises that he will multiply Abraham's seed – something that could not have happened if he had sacrificed his son. Yet Abraham betrayed the promise you make at the birth of your child: that you will look after him or her always, do everything so that your child will be happy throughout life.

What is a father?

A father is someone who is responsible for a being he has created. He must defend and help his child under all circumstances. A father might also be confronted with situations where he doesn't know what to do – as with Abraham when he was faced with God.

I looked in a dictionary, and saw that a father [père] was 'a man who engendered one or more children'. And then, by chance, my eye fell on the word 'to lose' [perdre].

Losing is what this story is about: Isaac loses his father and Abraham almost loses himself as a father, which he would have done if he had killed Isaac, but even if he doesn't kill him, he loses himself because Isaac no longer feels protected.

He can no longer trust his father [...].

⁓

When Anna had finished, it was, as for the other children, the turn of her parents to address her in public, before each gave her a symbolic gift in some way linked to the past.

Adine spoke of her love for Anna.

The gift she had chosen was a diamond set in a pendant. It had belonged to her own maternal grandmother, Suzanne.

Anna received it now, and kissed Adine.

There was a pause, then it was my turn.

On a low table I had placed the two objects I was going to give Anna, one of them wrapped in tinfoil.

I had written out what I intended to say, but now I did not want to read my notes.

On my thirteenth birthday, I began, and as I said these words it felt as if a great spinning had been set in motion inside me. I was standing on the stage with my wife and daughter, but I was simultaneously back in the Volkswagen with my father more than forty years earlier: the past came homing in on me with accelerating intensity and dovetailed in its flight with what was happening in the present.

I was a son, with my father relinquishing to me a man's responsibility. I was a father embracing my daughter on the threshold of her journey to womanhood, and still a son, in the severed, raw time of my thirteenth birthday.

One thing that had been missing then was the speech.

And before that the commentary.

There was no Hebrew, but we managed nonetheless.

No full congregation, though the one person who mattered most had, despite himself, been there with me.

It had not been much.

Yet all the same it was a rite of passage, as a bar mitzvah should be.

The best bar mitzvah possible, under the circumstances.

⌒

I gave Anna the first of the two objects I had brought
with me.

As she unwrapped it from the tinfoil some people in
the audience began laughing. Among the objects that
had been given to the other children as heirlooms were
a much-used pair of tailor's shears from someone's
grandfather; the big, old, rusty key to a house
somewhere in Poland that a great-grandmother had
fled from; a woven scarf passed down for generations
in southern France; and then my wife's diamond from
Saint Petersburg. So it was a bit strange for Anna to
now be producing a simple hen's egg.

Then she unwrapped the egg scale.

There she stood, with the diamond around her
neck from out of her Russian ancestry; a symbol of
fertility in one hand, a tool linking that symbol to
the material world in the other, both her maternal
grandmothers standing with us up there on the stage.

⌒

A few months before her bat mitzvah, when Anna
learned that the giving of symbolic gifts would be part

of the ceremony, instead of imagining what it was that she would receive, she asked: *I wonder which gifts I will give to my own children?*

Four

In 1971, the year I turned twenty, while we were still in Johannesburg, my brother Allen decided that since so many boys in his class were going to celebrate their bar mitzvahs, he would have one too. He went to weekly Hebrew lessons, followed by special bar mitzvah classes with the rabbi, in the orthodox synagogue next to the same school football field where I had once played.

I remember watching him, one Saturday morning in 1972, draped in a long, shiny white tallith, as he walked proudly across the red carpet of the synagogue towards the raised lectern, male members of the congregation to either side of him, women and girls gathered up in the gallery overhead. At his side was the rabbi, bearing the scrolls of the torah in its rich and embroidered velvet cover. Ben Baruch Hirson, the rabbi introduced him as: his father's son.

Following the rabbi's pointer, Allen read out, in the required singsong tones, a long passage from the holy text that he had spent days on end learning by rote.

The passage had been chosen from a list according to the date of the ceremony and happened to be the longest one available. He barely understood a single word of what he was saying.

The rabbi, who was from the United States, spoke of the way an olive must be crushed in order to yield its oil, and how it can be used as nourishment and a source of light. This was most likely an expression of oblique sympathy for my father, though I suppose he would only moderately have appreciated being compared to a crushed olive.

I was aware of my own heaviness, upright in the pews, as the chazzan started singing and his voice went through me like a swallow flying under the swollen bruise of storm clouds, drunk on the smell of rain, looping the grey weight of air with its song.

There was no marquee, little alcohol, no speech by my brother or anyone else. But there was a feast that took place later in the nearby flat that my Great-Aunt Essie now shared with her sister-in-law Bessie.

Had Granny Lily been there she would no doubt have done some incomparable baking; Grandpa Joe would most probably not have wanted to come. But no one would ever know for sure: Granny Lily had sadly passed away a few years earlier, and Joe followed her not long afterwards.

One last thing: my mother was there, unusually sociable, unrecognisably voluble, as she went around speaking to the roomful of guests. In her eyes I thought I saw a spark of triumph, struck by my brother who had pulled off this celebration for himself. Baruch, at that point, had been absent for almost eight years.

⁀

For his bar mitzvah my brother received from his mother, and nominally from his father, a smart Timex watch with phosphorescent hands, and displayed it on his wrist when he went, with his sister, for the one visit to their father during all his time in prison.

The visit took place in the office of Commanding Officer Schnepel, a man my mother and I had already seen strutting, potbelly first, around the front of the prison buildings, the curling tusks of a nicotine-coloured moustache against red cheeks that looked at if they were steaming. He was able to smile and scowl at the same time, and his mood was known to swing unpredictably from blunt condescension through brief, jovial indulgence to damning contempt.

He, too, was present during the visit. My father had brought along a roll of sweets, and every time he wanted to give one to my brother and sister, Schnepel reached out a hand to check that there was nothing hidden inside it.

My father mentioned none of this in the next letter home, sent on 12 April 1972, in his fine hand, on lined pale blue paper with the usual purple GEVANGENIS/ PRISON rubber stamp on the first page.

Instead, he wrote about his efforts, in the allotted forty minutes, to make contact with these two children whom he barely knew, attempting to discuss science, sport, the gaillardias he himself had grown and brought in a bunch from the prison garden.

But, according to him, it was Allen who did most of the talking while Zoë sat on her father's lap, evidently taking in this man she had last set eyes on when she was nine months old.

> Then all too soon, time was up. [Zoë's] little face lifted and brushed my lips for a warm kiss. A kiss too from Allen. And they left the room with me saying: It won't be long now... Waving arms of farewell from down the corridor, as I wandered back to routine again.

How many unspoken words were packed between the two syllables of the word 'routine'? Not the slightest description of prison conditions was allowed in those letters scoured, sometimes blotted out in places, and then signed by a censor.

He did not mention, either in this letter or on any other occasion as far as I know, that such a highly unusual visit was most probably applied for and granted on the occasion of my brother's thirteenth birthday.

Apart from that Timex watch, Allen also received for his bar mitzvah what amounted to a fine sum of money from various people, enough to buy a shiny blue sports bicycle with drop-down handlebars.

He once reminded me that I had expressed some jealousy at the time. This, he thought, had to do with the money. But it had nothing to do with money. It had to do with the event itself. Here was my younger brother dodging through the gap of my father's absence to do what he wanted, when, at his age, I might have almost wished for the same, had my father left me to my own devices.

Still, since my brother mentioned gifts to me, I could have told him that I, too, had received a good number of them during my special birthday visit. Enough to last a lifetime, though I was incapable of seeing them as gifts to begin with, quite the contrary, since they were enveloped in a wrapping of separation, and longing, and loss.

They were gifts, but of the kind that cannot be opened too early, like a fruit that is toxic if eaten unripe. So they had to be unwrapped slowly, over time, with care. Some were not, however, they were opened too quickly, and I took their poison when I was too young to know that I should spit it out before swallowing.

Yet even from that poison there was something to be learned, and it was in the learning that I was given them as gifts. So they might be called lessons, shaped by the time and place where they were to be learned as I came to the threshold of manhood.

Perhaps the least obvious of them, and yet the easiest to mention now, was the presence of the two policemen. I knew already that they were on the wrong side in a hidden war that my father had been engaged in. The whole front of the car was on the wrong side and I was close enough to it to see the pinkish, oily skin of those policemen's scalps under their shorn hair.

Then again, the back of the Volkswagen was on the wrong side too. My father was being held there, and for thirty minutes I, in my entirely porous state, absorbed his defeat.

We were in enemy territory. On my thirteenth birthday I had been invited, not into the heat of battle but to where the consequences of battle could be clearly seen.

Just outside that car, in Hillbrow, near the middle of town and even where we lived a brief journey away in Johannesburg's northern suburbs, among the cooing of doves and the burbling of swimming pools, somewhere under the deep blue empire of the sky there was a war hidden away. You needed to keep your eyes skinned if you wanted to see the barbed wire of the law, barely sticking through the comfortably padded fabric of our days.

There was a war, and there was peace, both existing separately at the same time and in the same place.

Next, as I have mentioned before, there was the presence of the car itself. Who celebrates a thirteenth birthday in a car, suspended about 25 centimetres above the ground, without anyone getting out at some point in the proceedings to get a drink or even stretch their legs? This was, in its own way, a gift: knowledge that the world before me rested not on rock but (if my luck did not run out) on rubber wheels. Any semblance of permanence could start sliding underfoot from one moment to the next, ready or not, on a birthday or any other day of any year to come.

For the moment, the Volkswagen was a sign that my father had been reduced to immobility. Considered from another perspective, it was also ultimately exactly the opposite. That car was ready to roll, and not in a direction chosen by either of us sitting on the back seat.

We knew it would be heading for the prison, less than a minute away, leaving me behind. But, had I only been able to foresee it, the journey was far longer than that car would be making. It would ultimately take my father into exile and the rest of our family with him, outwards, beyond the frontiers of any single country.

The worst gift of all, though, concerned my father and me. Who, on his thirteenth birthday, sees his father for the first time entirely unable to make the least decision concerning his own fate?

Could that possibly have been a gift? It was knowledge that love would most likely endure through the loved one's weakness, but also that even my towering father could topple, and if he could do so, then the same might happen to someone else. Anyone who was the light of your world might be summarily removed one day and walled off in darkness the next. So it was best to find one's own feet to stand on, though mine were pretty wobbly at the time.

I was an unworked-out, pimply boy with a broken front tooth who had just turned thirteen and still had the remnants of an English accent. I wanted to score a try for the under-thirteen A rugby team and play chess for our school. There was a girl I would have liked to kiss though the closest I got was writing who knows what in her little pastel-paged autograph book.

I wanted nothing better than to have my father back in his place. But his place was empty, unlikely to be filled again by him in a hurry. Was I, in the meantime, not being appointed stopgap, go-between, or even emissary?

Yes, I was.

Here is what my father later wrote about that moment:

I also tried, in a move that was over-subtle, to send a message to Yael via Denis. He could not have been expected to gather what I tried to say, and he did not. Whether I had the right to draw him into my devious scheme is dubious. In my keenness to see Denis, I had also made a grievous mistake. It was good to see him, and I savoured that brief contact. However I had not thought of the traumatic effect that visit might have on him. He had been placed in a situation of stress from which he should have been insulated.

From my father's point of view, something else was also going on during that visit. The pulsing I felt in his hand, probably just as he began asking me questions about my mother, was most likely to alert me to whatever he wanted to tell her.

Did something need to be hidden by her in case the Special Branch paid another visit to our house, or his university office? Was this anything to do with health, or conditions in his cell, or (though I doubt it) escape? Was it, perhaps, simply a message of love? (But then why would that have been a secret?)

One way or another, I will never know what that 'devious scheme' might have been. We never spoke about the visit while he was alive, nor did I read the lines I have just quoted from his autobiography before he died, or at least not carefully enough to realise that my special birthday visit may have been organised so that my father could communicate secretly with my mother.

Even if that was not the case, she may have been on his mind all the way through: he was, after all, a man in his early forties being held in solitary confinement, no doubt needing to reach in whatever way possible the woman he had seen only once or twice under highly strained circumstances since leaving for Durban five or six weeks earlier and was unlikely to be able to touch, or be with freely in any way, for years to come.

There she was, sitting in a car a dozen paces away though he could not go to her. Was her unattainable presence not a sign to him of his need and despair and checked potency? How much, for him, did the visit have to do with me?

This, then, was the ultimate gift: to understand that, in the thick of trouble, when sky and earth seemed to contract against my skin and lock me into myself, there were nonetheless other people involved in the same event, quite possibly even more distressed than I was, their hearts beating differently from my own, their minds working along quite different pathways.

With just a millimetre of distance from what was going on, I might have noticed my father's intention, taken a step back from my own need. But distance was what I lacked entirely; that most precious of gifts was inaccessible to me then and for far too long afterwards.

⌒

It was 25 August 1964, a cool, crisp afternoon towards the end of winter. Buds, each one sheathed in overlapping, minute dry scales, knotted the twigs of plane trees along the streets of the city.

I turned to see the Volkswagen driving away, back to the prison gate, but could no longer make out my father inside it. Yet during the time of that visit in the parking lot, a mark was gashed onto the map of my mind, as if to say: *pay attention, this is kilometre zero of the inner journey you will have to make one day.*

Travel as far away as you wish, but still you will need to come back here.

Take possession of this place, and it will flower with the blazing cold heat of belonging.

Because no root runs deeper than one that passes through the wound of love.

Afterword

The parking lot where I visited my father in late August 1964 is still there, though it seems smaller, and is no longer tarred but covered in greyish paving stones. The great old wooden door that once led to the prison is there, too, so are many of the old prison buildings. But the whole place has radically changed. It is now known as Constitution Hill. No one has been detained there since 1983. In a new building constructed out of bricks from a demolished wing of the one-time prison, judges gather to deliberate in South Africa's Constitutional Court.

You can visit the room where this happens, see preserved parts of the Old Fort, pause to read the names of prisoners who have since become famous; learn something of the place's past and from which sections of the population the prisoners came, one restlessly discontented generation of them after another, decade after decade, scooped from out of the rough and often violent cross-currents of local history.

First among them were rowdy miners, no doubt stoked with alcohol, held for disrupting the camp of gold-seekers that had given dusty, chaotic birth to Johannesburg in 1886; then miners again, striking for the rights of a white trade union, later striking once more in the face of bosses threatening to ditch them for dirt-cheap black labour.

British soldiers clad in red were taken prisoner there while battling for the infant city's gold to go to Empire. Next, Boers with gaunt, stubbled faces who had fought back and been defeated by those same soldiers; then their bitter descendants, rebelling against the country's entry into World War One on the side of the British. A generation later they were locked up for doing the same during World War Two.

In another section of the prison: blacks, both men and women, caught wandering the streets without a pass, or brewing white lightning, or found out by an abrupt shaft of torchlight at dawn sleeping with no legal permission at the side of a loved one.

Added to this motley crowd: in separated sections of the prison, blacks and whites, amongst them my father, awaiting trial for having taken up arms so that those people constantly pursued and humiliated and used might at last live in a country where they could hope to walk freely.

I know all this partly because one day, while I was in Johannesburg in July 2006, I received an invitation to go back to the Old Fort. I had not wanted to return, but despite myself I accepted, taking with me my wife and two children. I left them at a café table out in the winter sunshine of what had been the prison courtyard, then headed for the weakly lit corridors of one of the old prison buildings.

A series of doors, each of them four fingers thick and fitted with the slot of a judas eye, opened into the cells.

I entered one of them.

The floor was of black slate, the door had bolts that bit into the iron plating of its inner side. The walls were glazed with grey paint to above head height, then dirty cream to the ceiling. Words of anxiety and deprivation were scratched against them, one or two sweet names of hope, and a single quote: 'Cry O beloved country, for the unborn child who is going to inherit our fear.'

Well beyond reach, a barred window, cutting a rectangle out of the sky.

I stood there and my stomach muscles turned hard as a shield.

The Volkswagen where I had sat with my father was an antechamber to this place, but, after he had left, I shut out the possibility of following him further, even in my imagination, and the memory of that clenched refusal had remained in my body.

I walked back from the cell towards the courtyard, and for hours afterwards I was still breathing out of me the old numb sense of loss and desolation.

⁀

My special thirteenth birthday visit was over.

As my father was driven off towards the prison I walked upslope about a dozen paces, entering the car where my mother and her friend had been waiting.

For me that afternoon the world seemed to have stopped in its circuit through space. Which was of course not the case. It never is. Even on a windless day when not a single leaf trembles on the trees and it is difficult to believe that the sky and the earth are not curved in perfect immobility against each other, nonetheless the world does not stop turning.

Everything during those thirty minutes in the car had seemed to be arrested, all of space frozen into the shape of a round-backed, four-wheeled vehicle. Yet the whole wide world was spinning as always, and time was washing it as it spun, great slopes of time irrepressible as the waves of any ocean, rocking and rising, colliding and smoothing themselves against the sides of the world as we drove away from the prison, across the parking lot and into the stream of mid-afternoon traffic.

Notes

p.11 Ani rotze (I would like) and bevakasha (please): words transliterated from the Hebrew.

p.13 The Mau Mau uprising against the British authorities in Kenya (1952–1960) was regularly and dramatically covered by the South African press.

p.19 *Ops us a sarmie* was slang at the time for 'let me have a sandwich'.

p.43 There were several white miners' strikes in Johannesburg in the first decades of the twentieth century. The one in question, the biggest and most violent of them, continued from December 1921 (when my father was born) until March 1922.

p.64 Cato Manor: a township just outside Durban. In 1959 there was a wave of rioting and destruction of state property as black residents resisted the destruction of their homes and property.

Robert Sobukwe: prominent black South African political leader, founder of the Pan Africanist Congress.

Albert Luthuli: president of the African National Congress, awarded the Nobel Peace Prize in 1960.

p.77 In August 1963, after bribing a policeman, Arthur Goldreich and Harold Wolpe escaped from the Marshall Square prison cells in Johannesburg, both of them disguised as priests, and were able to leave the country. I do not remember any mention being made on the British television news of two other men, Mosie Moola and Abdulhay Jassat, who escaped at the same time.

p.83 See Roscow, G.H. 'What is "Sumer is icumen in?"', *The Review of English Studies*, New Series, 50, 198 (1999), 188–195.

p.105 For an account of my father's detention at the Old Fort, see his autobiography: Hirson, B. *Revolutions in My Life*. Johannesburg: Wits University Press, 1995, pp.328–331.

The General Law Amendment Act number 37 of 1963 allowed a person suspected of a political crime to be detained without a warrant for up to ninety days without access to a lawyer, and then, if the person was released, to be immediately re-detained for the same period.

pp.106–108 According to the 1960 census (which underestimated the black population by not counting those in the 'Homelands'), there were 17,100,000 people in South Africa, less than 20 per cent of them white. Only whites could vote. Concerning those parties which represented the majority in one way or another, the African National Congress (ANC) and Pan Africanist Congress (PAC) were both banned in 1960. The Communist Party had been banned in 1950. The Liberal Party disbanded in 1968.

An account of the trial is recorded in Hugh Lewin's book *Bandiet Out of Jail* (originally published as *Bandiet*). Johannesburg: Random House, 2002, pp.53–55; also in Baruch Hirson, *Revolutions In My Life*. Op cit, 331–335.

p.110 Snaith, S. 'Pylons'. *The Silver Scythe*. London: Blythenhale Press, 1933.

p.111 Lewin, Hugh. 'Pylon', *Bandiet Out of Jail*, p.204. On my father's doubts concerning the strategy of sabotage, see his *Revolutions In My Life*, pp.301 and 321–323.

pp.112–113 My conversations with Raymond Eisenstein and Bernice Laschinger took place in 2018. I met Raymond in a discreet corner of a chic Paris brasserie; Bernice spoke to me on the phone from London.

p.115 Among the men we met on their release from prison were Lewis Baker, Raymond Eisenstein, Issy Heymann, John Laredo, Hugh Lewin and Ivan Schermbrucker.

p.121 The four quotes are, respectively, from Psalm 22, Psalm 8, Matthew Ch.5 v.15, and I Corinthians Ch.13 v.12.

p.143 Cavafy, C.P. 'The City'. Keeley, E. and Philip, S. *Four Greek Poets*. London: Penguin, 1966, p.13.

p.145 For the link between identity and story-telling, see Huston, N. *The Tale-Tellers: A Short History of Humankind*. Toronto: McArthur & Company, 2008.

p.149 My wife's mother, Avital Sagalyn, can be seen and heard telling the story of her family's escape from Brussels in a film made by her son Daniel: https://youtu.be/uyW1psSlTHE

The full text of my mother Yael Hirson's story was reprinted in my book *White Scars*. Johannesburg: Jacana Media, 2006, p.163.

p.155 'Baruch was a one-man struggle' is what Haleh Afshar said while speaking at the Institute for Commonwealth Studies, London, on 14 October 2000, during the memorial meeting following my father's death. The text of her talk is included in the privately printed booklet, *In Memory of Baruch Hirson 1921–1999.*

p.160 David Webster was shot dead in front of his Johannesburg home on 1 May 1989.

Rick Turner, shot in his Durban home on the night of 8 January 1978, died in the arms of his daughter Jann.

Jenny Curtis was killed along with her daughter Katryn on opening a letter-bomb in her home in Lubango, northern Angola, on 28 June 1984.

p.162 The Cercle Bernard Lazare is a secular association named for a nineteenth-century socialist writer who gave significant support to the cause of Alfred Dreyfus, and is linked with both the Israeli Peace Now activist group and the socialist youth movement Hashomer Hatzair.

p.163 I have translated Anna's text from the original French.

p.165 Arnold von Gennep, writer of the classic anthropological work on rites of passage, *The Rites of Passage,* describes three possible stages a rite of puberty could go through. Firstly, a separation from the social world of before; secondly, the initiate's entry into that liminal space sometimes known as no man's land. Here the rite itself takes place, with its officiants, their acts and accoutrements, the lessons they teach in order to prepare the initiate for the next stage of life. Thirdly, there is the initiate's re-entry into the outside world, in a newly altered state. These three stages would seem to correspond perfectly to my thirteenth-birthday prison visit. Von Gennep. *The Rites of Passage*. London: Routledge & Kegan Paul, 1908, reprinted 1977.

p.173 For the etymological relationship between the words 'gift' and 'poison', see https://www.etymonline.com/word/poison: 'In many Germanic languages "poison" is named by a word equivalent to the English "gift" (such as Old High German *gift*, German *Gift*, Danish and Swedish *gift*; Dutch *gift, vergift,* [Afrikaans *gif*]. This shift might have been partly euphemistic, partly by influence of the Greek *dosis*, "a portion prescribed", literally "a giving", used by Galen and other Greek physicians to mean an amount of medicine.'

p.177 For my father's mention of the special thirteenth-birthday visit, see *Revolutions In My Life*, p.330.

p.183 'Cry O beloved country, for the unborn child who is going to inherit our fear': an (imperfect) quote from Alan Paton's *Cry, the Beloved Country*.

Acknowledgements

This little book has gone through more drafts than I care to remember, over more years than I care to name. It was begun well before the coronavirus first threw its mortal veil over the world; I went on rewriting it through three lockdowns in France, and then all over again when I learned that it would finally be published.

Its life on the computer screen might have been considerably shorter had Adine Sagalyn not refused to allow me to say, for many months on end, that the manuscript was completed. She went on to point out precisely why. Without her, I doubt that I would have broached some of the most difficult passages involved in this account.

Thanks to Robert Berold for the magic scalpel of his editorial work, and to Nina Bogin for her wise accompaniment of the MS in its final stages.

Thanks also to Stephen Clingman, Nancy Huston, Antoine Lermuzeaux and Jenny Rose for their incisively critical yet generous reading of the MS in its infancy and at other points in its life cycle.

Thanks to Anne-Christine Le Gendre for an

essential conversation that opened some rusty old doors.

Thanks to Bernice Laschinger and Raymond Eisenstein for invaluable information.

Thanks to Oded Eldad, sad thanks, since he died in 2020. Oded accompanied our children Anna and Jeremy wonderfully during their respective bat mitzvah and bar mitzvah. His conception of this ceremony contributed to changing my vision of what had happened to me on my thirteenth birthday.

Thanks to the Heinrich and Jane Ledig-Rowohlt Foundation, to Ellen Hinsey, and Sophie Kandaouroff of the Chateau de Lavigny, where a very early draft of this book was begun.

Thanks to Isobel Dixon, my agent, for taking on this book in turbulent times. Thanks to Bridget Impey and Maggie Davey of Jacana Media for wanting to publish this book so promptly and enthusiastically. And thanks to Shay Heydenrych, Lara Jacob and Alison Lowry for their meticulous work.

Thanks to Adam Freudenheim of Pushkin Press for so energetically wanting to take this book beyond the borders of South Africa, and to Rory Williamson of the same publishing house for his help.

Thanks above all to my daughter Anna. This book would never have been written had she not, at the age of eleven, brought me back to looking closely at my relationship with my father.